Praise for *My Best Race*

"We all have our own favorite race stories but Chris Cooper has selected fifty such tales from runners of all abilities, and through his artful choreography has made them inspiring, riveting, moving, at times funny, and always compelling. Whether you are getting ready for your twentieth marathon or your first 5K, you should make this book part of your training plan. It will put a smile on your face, make you dig down deeper and perhaps, even run a little faster."
– George A. Hirsch, Chairman of the New York Road Runners and former publisher of *Runner's World*

"I found the book fascinating and loved reading about the thoughts we all go through before, during and after a race. This would be a great gift, or simply a good read for you to learn from the successes and mistakes that every runner makes."
– Lisa Rainsberger, 2-time winner of the Chicago Marathon and the last American woman to win the Boston Marathon

"*My Best Race* is a brilliant idea for a book that's well written and a compelling read from start to finish. It provides a fresh look at competitive running, and surprises and motivates with a lesson in every chapter."
– Jon Sinclair, former USA Cross Country and 10K champion

"What a fascinating concept! *My Best Race* is a very unique and inspiring collection that gives great insight into the minds of runners."
– Keith Brantly, member of the 1996 US Olympic Marathon team

For Marion

Diversion Books
A Division of Diversion Publishing Corp.
443 Park Avenue South, Suite 1008
New York, New York 10016
www.DiversionBooks.com

For more information, email info@diversionbooks.com

First Diversion Books edition August 2013.
Print ISBN: 978-1-62681-599-5
eBook ISBN: 978-1-62681-016-7

MY
BEST
RACE

50 Runners and the Finish Line They'll Never Forget

Edited by Chris Cooper

DIVERSIONBOOKS

Contents

I have fought the good fight,
I have finished the race,
I have kept the faith.

2 Timothy 4:7

Introduction

According to Running USA, there were more than fifteen million road race finishers in the United States in the past year, the ninth consecutive annual increase. They raced for the challenge, for the achievement, for the health benefits, and for many other personal reasons. But whether they were twenty-mile-a-day elite marathoners or twenty-mile-a-week recreational runners, each of them can invariably point to a singular performance recently or in their past as *"the best race I ever ran."*

My Best Race is a collection of those singular performances. In this inspirational book, fifty runners, from Olympians and World Champions, to courageous disabled athletes and middle-of-the-packers, share their personal accounts of what they consider the best race they ever ran … and why. Was it the race that helped their team to a championship? Was it the race that qualified them for the Olympics? Or was it not necessarily one in which they ran their fastest or placed the highest? Indeed, many consider their best race less in terms of awards or accolades and more in terms of how that achievement—win or lose—transformed their lives. Take Ed Eyestone for example. How he fared at a high school cross-country meet instilled in him the confidence to one day become an NCAA champion and two-time Olympian. For him, the sheer joy he felt in that nearly forgotten local race was just as thrilling as what he experienced in his more public triumphs on the world stage.

Olympic torch bearer John Stanton says that a race should become not a test but a celebration because of the lifetime of memories it can create. "Often the memory is not just about running the race itself," he says, "but about the people you meet or the experiences within the race that are so special. It's those little touch points we have."

The races described on the following pages are the ones these famous and not-so-famous runners say they keep coming back to at various points in their lives for sustenance, assurance, and comfort—or just to bring a smile to their face. Many were recalled with excitement, some with laughter, others with tears. And just as these athletes admitted how much they enjoyed reliving these special races with me in our interviews, I enjoyed listening to them and bringing their stories to you. I hope these stories inspire you to run your best race, if you haven't run it already.

Chris Cooper
August 2013

Kara Goucher

Kara and her son at the finish of the half-marathon

"There's a point in a race where you're on the edge and you're pushing so hard and you're riding this line and if you push a little too much you're going to blow up, but if you keep riding that line something special can happen." On June 16, 2012 something special *did* happen to Kara Goucher on the streets of Duluth, Minnesota. Not all of it involved her setting a course record, however. The Olympian had finally returned home to give something back to her community, and in the end they gave something back to her as well.

Kara Goucher was only six years old when she first displayed the spunk and determination needed to win three NCAA championships and berths on two Olympic teams. "I ran

11

my first race with my grandfather when I was six," she says. "He took me to this local one mile race and I got tripped at the start and had a bloody knee. He picked me up and thought I'd just want to return home because I was a real girlie girl. Instead I'm told I said, 'Let's go! We're getting beat already!'" Still it would be many more years before Kara would begin running regularly. "In junior high I decided to try for the Triple 'A' Award," she recalls. "You had to have a certain GPA for academics, you had to do an art (she was in the band), and you had to do athletics. The two athletic options at my school were volleyball and cross-country running. I tried hitting the volleyball and my wrist hurt so bad I thought there was no way I was going to make that team. The cross-country team was meeting the next day and I heard they didn't cut anybody, so I joined. My un-athleticism actually worked out for me."

Kara continued running in high school, and in her freshman year she beat a state champion and earned a spot at the state championships for the two-mile run. Eventually she realized just how far running could take her. "I liked winning," she says. "I was never particularly good at anything, so for me to be able to win some races was pretty cool. In my sophomore year I qualified for the Foot Locker National Cross-Country Championships and got to ride on a plane to San Diego when it was snowing back home in Duluth. Then I learned in the hotel I didn't have to share a bed like at the state meets when we were crammed all together. For the first time in my life I felt that running was something really special and something that could take me places."

At the University of Colorado Kara was a three-time NCAA champion, but her racing career was interrupted by injuries her senior year and for the next three years after signing with Nike as a professional. "I only raced once or twice a year due to injury and thought about retiring," she recalls. "I really struggled with the transition from college to pro." Once she was injury free and under the tutelage of coach Alberto Salazar, however, she blossomed as an elite runner on the international stage and competed in the Beijing Olympics in both the 5,000 meters (3.1

miles) and 10,000 meters (6.2 miles). "I began training more like a professional," she remembers. "That whole lifestyle of getting massages and lifting weights really turned things around for me. Then Alberto convinced me to try the marathon and I loved it and really enjoyed the training and the whole process. I grew up watching Grandma's Marathon in Duluth and would hand out water to the runners and cheer on my friends, but I thought they were all crazy to run that far and I would never do that." But she did, and when Kara finished third in the 2008 New York City Marathon, it was the fastest marathon debut ever by an American woman.

Four years later after taking time off to give birth to her son, Kara was back in top form and had a decision to make. Having qualified for the 2012 Olympics in the marathon, she was given the option by her new coach, Jerry Schumacher, of going to the Olympic Trials to run the 10,000 meters or to Duluth to compete in the USA Half Marathon (13.1 miles) Championship. The race was to be run in conjunction with the annual Garry Bjorklund Half Marathon. "For me it was a no-brainer," she says. "I was already on the Olympic team in the marathon, and I rarely got to go home and never got to race at home. For my hometown to be hosting the championship was amazing. Duluth had supported me so much over the years and I wanted to show them how much it had meant to me. I wanted to not only win but break the course record to show everyone in Duluth that, of all the runners and Olympians who have come through there from all different countries, the girl who grew up there was the fastest."

The half marathon would be Kara's only race before the London Olympics in August, and her coach did not want to ease off in her training. A typical workout for the thirty-four-year-old past and future Olympian? Running for forty-five minutes at six-minute-per-mile pace before "cutting down" to 5:30 pace over the next forty-five minutes. "I was running a lot of miles," she recalls. "I was doing about 100 to 120 miles a week and I knew that, without a taper, the half marathon was going to be tough." Kara arrived a few days before the race and stayed at her mother's house outside Duluth. From there she drove into town to reacquaint herself with a running route that would once again play a big role in her life. "Two days before the race I ran the last four miles to remind myself of that part of the course. It was right down the street from my high school and I had run on those roads literally thousands of times. There were so many memories of that place where I fell in love with running; it was very emotional for me to go back. And it was almost surreal to be running professionally at a place where I had run so many times growing up."

"Kara, you went to high school with my daughter!" The well-wishers greeted the hometown girl from the minute she arrived in the warm-up area to long after the race had ended. "It was hard for me to even do my warm-ups," she recalls, "because all these people wanted to tell me they knew me or remind me that they knew me or that I was in English class with their son, but it was really fun. Literally on the starting line it was like, 'Hey, Kara, you ran the relay in high school with my daughter!' I was thinking, 'I'm about to run a race, you can't come talk to me right now.' It was crazy, but crazy in the best way. It didn't annoy me in the least."

Besides not being able to taper her workouts before the race, Kara had been concerned about a sore heel that was bothering her. But once the race began, her focus was more on her pace than anything else. "The course record was seventy minutes, which is exactly 5:20 per mile, and I didn't want to go out too fast at the beginning and put a target on my back. My coach said to stop worrying about the course record—he just wanted me to run smart. But the girls went out hard at 5:15 for the first mile and I thought, 'Oh my gosh, no one's going to hand this race to me. I would have to earn it.' That was actually good because we got into a good rhythm right away and the pace did start to sag a little bit. I just wanted to run with people as long as possible until I felt confident I could make a move. I ran with a group for about five miles, and then it was just me and Maegan Krifchin until about eight miles. I could see then that if I didn't start after the course record it wasn't going to happen, so that's when I decided to take a risk and put myself out there and go for it. I calculated I had to average 5:15 from there on out in order to run seventy minutes. It was a pretty significant change of pace at that point and I was able to put some distance between myself and Maegan."

Just as it was before the race, the locals continued their outpouring of support for Kara along each mile. "It was just amazing," she says. "There were signs with my name on it and people were so funny. There was this group of guys that yelled, 'You don't know us but we went to high school with you!' One person even ran alongside me and said, 'Hey, Kara, you probably don't remember me but you ran with my daughter.' I had to tell him, 'I'm racing right now!'"

But any levity she experienced along the course was soon replaced by the mental and physical stress she faced in order to sustain, but not exceed, that demanding pace. "It was tough and I was tired," she recalls after reaching eleven miles. "I was definitely riding that line and breathing hard. I ran past my coach who said, 'You've got to dig now, make it hurt,' and that really motivated me. Since I missed the split time at the twelve-mile mark I didn't know if I was going to get the record or not; I just knew I was running hard. At that point I was hurting. Before I was trying to look good for everybody on the course, but at that point I was starting to run 'ugly' but there was a good reason for it; at the end I learned I was running at 5:08 pace."

Near the end of the half marathon course the runners navigate a turn in the road before getting a view of the finish line 150 yards in the distance. "My form wasn't as good as I would have liked it to be because I was running as hard as I could," she says. "The crowds were really big but all I could think about was the time. I was still too far away to see the clock, but finally it came into focus and I realized I was going to get the record. I started sprinting as hard as I could, and I remember I just roared when I crossed the line because I was so pumped!" Kara's wining time for the 13.1-mile race was 1:09:46, a course record by fourteen seconds.

"At the finish were all these people from my past. My high

school coach was there and my cross-country teammates, and my family, and my grandparents who were crying. They all literally saw me grow up running on my first team as a twelve-year-old and were there through thick and thin for me. To come back twenty-two years later and still be running was like coming full circle for me. It was the highlight of my career finishing that race in front of everybody that I love who had been there from the beginning before I was anything special. And it was just so much fun. I had the time of my life out there on the course with all those people. It was a thing of pride for the community and it was an unbelievable thing for me. I've never felt so loved and embraced, and that's why it was the best race I've ever run."

Running Tip: "It's just about running for all the right reasons and choosing your races for the right reasons. I think when you make decisions based on your heart, more often than not it works out in the best way possible and you appreciate the journey so much more."

Jeff Galloway

With a quarter mile to go in the Olympic Trials marathon, Jeff Galloway and Jack Bachelor were tied for third place. Unfortunately, only the top three finishers would earn a coveted spot on that 1972 team; in the harsh reality of Olympic qualifying, fourth place is as good as last. "When we entered the stadium for the finish, the crowd saw two people together with only one spot left on the team," says Jeff, "but I was in perfect control over the situation."

Jeff's 140-mile training weeks, with a long run of up to thirty miles every third week, had prepared him perfectly for that race, endowing him with the physical strength and mental toughness needed to compete at the highest level of competition in the grueling 26.2-mile contest. It was no surprise, therefore, to see him on the cusp of making the Olympic team. By contrast, Jack was not expected to be among the leaders so late in the race. The 10,000-meter (10K) specialist, struggling just to hold the pace, had focused his training more on quarter-mile speed workouts than high mileage; his longest run leading up to the race had been just 18 miles. Recalling the situation as they entered the final straightaway, Jeff says, "I felt wonderful. I was at the top of my powers and Jack was really pretty much exhausted."

Distance runners learn early on, however, that nothing is ever a sure thing. Even in the shortest races, something beyond their control—a cramp, a heat wave, a loss of confidence—can turn a dream into a nightmare. If Jeff really was "in perfect control over the situation," why did he suddenly fade at the end to finish fourth? And why does he still consider it the best race he ever ran?

Today, Jeff Galloway is a highly regarded running coach and author of some of the most popular books on running ever published. And while he was arguably in the best shape of his career back in 1972, he was anything *but* fit as a teenager. "I was a fat kid," he says, "and the reason I even got into running was because I had to choose a winter sport in high school." Learning that the cross-country coach was the most lenient in the athletic department, the choice was easy. "On the first day we just told him we were going to run on a trail, then all we had to do was jog into the woods and hide out." The strategy worked for a while until the day a friend made Jeff tag along with the serious runners; it was a day that changed his life. "I was pulled along by the energy of those runners," he recalls vividly, "and I knew it was something I wanted to do. Ever since then I wanted to be part of a running group."

Throughout high school and college, Jeff learned the value of being a part of the running fraternity, and when the decision came for graduate school, he enrolled at the University of Florida so he could join the newly formed Florida Track Club. The founder of the club was Jack Bachelor, and another member was Frank Shorter, who would eventually become one of the most successful and popular runners in the United States. "Jack was our mentor," says Jeff. "When things got tough he would kick us in the butt, but he was also patient and understanding. It was just a fun time and he was a fun person."

With a focus on the upcoming Olympic Trials, Frank Shorter found some inexpensive housing in Vail, Colorado and invited Jeff and Jack along so they could all train at altitude. "I was always grateful for that opportunity," says Jeff. "I felt that training significantly improved my performance." Indeed, after returning from Vail, Jeff ran a 10K race two minutes faster than his previous best time, giving him the confidence to enter the Olympic Trials at that distance as well as in the marathon. "The marathon was the better event for me and my best opportunity to make the Olympic team," he says, "but I wouldn't miss the opportunity to at least compete in the 10K trial."

No one was more surprised than Jeff when, after seven

laps, he found himself in third place behind Frank Shorter and Jack Bachelor. "It was about ninety degrees in Eugene, Oregon that day at the start of the 10K trial, and I was in last place for the first mile. But I had trained in Florida and was used to the heat, so I took my time and didn't exert myself early in the race. Then I noticed a guy in front of me slowing down so I passed him. Sure enough, someone else was slowing down so I passed him too." As other runners faded in the heat, Jeff caught and passed them until he was in third place. "That was the first time I realized I was really in the mix for the Olympic Games. It was an exhilarating experience. Then I caught up with Jack and passed him and finished second. It was the greatest surprise I ever had."

But the storybook ending of club mates Frank Shorter first, Jeff Galloway second, and Jack Bachelor third was not to be; Jack was passed by another runner near the finish. According to Jeff, however, there was a simple solution that would enable Jack to make the squad. "I would drop off the 10K team," says Jeff, "and allow Jack to move up from fourth to third place and qualify. After all, I still had a good chance to make the team in the marathon—that was a better event for me." But instead of finishing fourth, Jack was not even listed in the final results. In a ruling that remains questionable to this day, he was disqualified from the race for swerving out of his lane and accidentally bumping that passing runner.

Now the only remaining chance for Jack to make the Olympic team was in the marathon a week later. But he had two things working against him at that distance. Since he wasn't planning to run the marathon, his longest run leading up to the trials had been only eighteen miles, which, at an elite race level, is not enough. Also, according to Jeff, Jack tended to go out too fast like he did in that 10K race, and as he had done in his previous marathons. "Jack was so down," says Jeff.

But from his high school days running cross-country, to the camaraderie of the Florida Track Club, and to his recent training camp in the mountains of Vail, Jeff had grasped a valuable lesson. He knew the friendships formed in those groups are more important than how fast or how far one can run. "I had learned that running is the type of experience that can be enriched by the associations with other people, and it's even greater when you have a chance to share the wealth of things we get from running with a friend. So I told Jack I would take the responsibility of pacing him through the Olympic Trials marathon.

"My greatest asset at the time was pacing, I was a pacing metronome. I just developed a keen sense of pace honed through years of workouts on the track. I could estimate my time within a tenth of a second per lap. We ran together each day that next week going over what pace we thought would be enough to qualify in another hot race because the projected temperature for the day of the marathon was getting higher and higher." Similar to the strategy he used so successfully in the 10K trial, Jeff set a conservative pace due to the extreme heat. "We started out in about 100th place," says Jeff. "At about five miles we were in fiftieth, and we just steadily moved up because the others had gone out too fast. But once we got to about fifteen miles, Jack began to tire. We just kept talking about the runners still ahead of us and where we thought we could pass the next person." With five miles to go in the race, Jeff and Jack passed one more runner to move into third place.

"The last five miles was a bizarre experience," says Jeff. "By then we were on our own because Frank Shorter and Kenny Moore were a couple of minutes ahead of us and would eventually finish first and second. I felt strong but Jack was having a few doubts and didn't think he could maintain the pace. He did slow down in several places and kept asking me to look around to make sure no one was coming up on us. I tried to calm him and be positive. I became the lookout, the cheerleader, the confessor, you name it, and we held everybody off. As we crossed the river with about a mile to go, Jack perked up and started to regain some confidence, and when we entered the stadium both of us were buoyed by the crowd. Of course, I was feeling a whole lot better than he was, and he had to keep telling me to slow down. We stayed together right on to the finish, and

I dropped back at the finish line so he could qualify. It was a wonderful experience."

Things were not so wonderful for Jeff that September in Munich, where he failed to advance out of the preliminary round in the Olympic 10K. "The three who qualified out of my heat broke the Olympic record," he says. "Quite honestly, I was not at that level in the 10K." Those on the US marathon team, however, exceeded expectations, as Frank Shorter won the gold medal, Kenny Moore claimed fourth place, and Jack Bachelor finished ninth. The 1–4–9 finish remains the best performance ever by US marathoners in Olympic history. Knowing the marathon was his best race, that he was in the best shape of his career, and that he was a favorite to qualify for the Olympic team in the marathon, does Jeff Galloway ever think about what could have been? "I had no doubts from the very beginning that I was going to help Jack qualify at the trials. Yes, the marathon would have been the better event for me than the 10K, but the ability to help a friend do something that was really significant to him gave me this wonderful glow inside that exists to this day."

Running Tip: "Insert walk breaks into your training and racing to reduce injury and allow you to perform better in long distance events. Walk breaks allow runners to shift back and forth between walking and running muscles to help distribute the workload. Running muscles are less likely to become fatigued, while performance capacity improves. Once a runner finds the ideal ratio of running and walking for a given distance (see jeffgalloway.com), walk breaks allow him or her to stay strong all the way to the finish line."

Donald Arthur

Somewhere on the Verrazano-Narrows Bridge, among 32,000 other runners plodding through the first mile of the New York City Marathon, Donald Arthur came to an abrupt stop. "I didn't know what was happening," said Mack Andrews, Donald's running partner that day. "I was afraid something was wrong with him."

Three years earlier, there definitely *was* something wrong with Donald Arthur. "I was suffering from cardiomyopathy and my condition had worsened," he says. "My cardiologist said if I didn't get a heart transplant within six months I would die. I came home that day from the doctor's office and prayed that God would give me a second chance, but in order for that to happen I knew someone else would have to die, and that was the sad part." Donald will never forget the day he received the phone call informing him a donor heart had been found. "I stood there with the phone in my hand and started to cry," he says. "Who was it? What was this person like? What did they do? Was it someone's father or brother or sister?"

Donald didn't know it at the time, but the organ donor was a shooting victim with a big brother named Mack Andrews. The transplant of that twenty-five-year-old heart into Donald's fifty-two-year-old body was certainly a wake-up call. "I asked myself what I had done with my life up until then and the answer was 'nothing.' Now through the transplant I was given that second chance, and I owed it to the donor and his family to get out of my comfort zone and see what I could achieve." One way of doing that was through running, and once fully recovered, he visited the local Achilles International chapter. Achilles International is a nonprofit where able-bodied volunteers and people with disabilities come together to train for running events in an environment of support and community. There Donald listened to the stories and accomplishments of blind runners, runners on crutches, runners with no legs in wheelchairs, and how they not only kept active, but did marathons too. "With all those people, the words, 'I can't, we can't, don't exist," he says. "From then on, I knew I belonged. I was blessed with a second chance through my heart transplant, and Achilles International was giving me another chance as well."

Having never run before, Donald was definitely out of his comfort zone. Through supervised training and running at night and on weekends with Achilles' volunteers, however, he was well on his way to achieving a goal he never thought possible of "just being able to finish a race." Donald finished his first race, then another, and another, and has since completed forty-two marathons in thirty-two states at a brisk race-walking pace. But even with a new passion for marathons, and a new heart to replace the old one, there was another void left to fill: meeting his donor's family and expressing his gratitude. Initial attempts at contacting the family were unsuccessful until Mack Andrews saw a CNN story about a runner with a heart transplant who had just completed the 1998 New York City Marathon, and made the connection. Donald still has the letter Mack wrote suggesting they meet, and they have been friends ever since. The donor, Donald learned, was named Fitzgerald, but everyone called him "Poochie." "He was full of life and one of the funniest people I ever knew," says Mack. He never got into trouble, but one day he was just in the wrong place at the wrong time."

Meeting the donor's family, hearing the donor's story, making a lifelong friendship; the story could have ended there with all the loose ends neatly tied up. But then Mack Andrews had an idea: "Next time I'm going to do it with you," he told Donald.

The "it" Mack referred to was the 1999 New York City Marathon. "I was in the military and was used to long road marches, so I thought I could get through it," he says. And that was how they happened to be together that November day in 1999, on the Verrazano-Narrows Bridge, less than a mile into the New York City Marathon. And that was where Donald abruptly stopped. An injury? Out of breath? A problem with his heart? No, in fact, just the opposite. All he had needed was a few hundred yards to warm up and get the blood flowing. "I didn't know what to think," says Mack. "Then all of a sudden Donald took my hand and put it underneath his shirt and said, 'Feel your brother's heart.' I could feel my brother's heart beating and that was amazing! From then on I felt as though my brother was actually there, that he was still alive! And from that point on I felt it was the three of us: Donald, me, and Poochie." Donald agrees: "There were two of us out there running, but there was a third person no one could see, and that was his brother."

There were still more than twenty-five miles to cover in the race, but that only meant more time for them to savor the unique bond they shared. "We were talking and laughing … and crying a little bit too," says Donald. "We got to know each other better, and Mack told me all about his brother and what he was like. We just had a great time all the way through." Waiting for them at the finish was Poochie's mother. "I walked up to her and handed her my finisher's medal," says Donald. "After all, they showed through their tragedy that they were willing to give me the special gift of their loved one's heart. But she wouldn't take it. Instead she put it back around my neck," he says, his voice quivering. "That was the moment. It was quite a day."

Running marathons is not Donald's only achievement. Rather, it is a platform from which he helps promote organ and tissue donation. "It's my way of saying 'thank you' to donor families who have given so much, and a way of encouraging those waiting for transplants that there is hope." Donald remains active with the New York Organ Donor Network, and spreads the word about organ donation by giving talks in schools and communities throughout New York City.

And through it all, Poochie's heart is still going strong.

Running Tip: "You've got to *believe* that you can do it. You may not be the fastest runner, but maybe you can jog or walk or combine jogging and walking. If you believe, you're always in it, and you can achieve your goal."

John Stanton

John Stanton is fond of long races. The founder of the Running Room, a popular running-store chain in Canada, has completed over sixty marathons in his career, as well as the Canadian Ironman and the Ironman World Championship. One might find it surprising, therefore, to learn that John's best and most emotional race was actually the *shortest* race he ever ran. On a cold and blustery winter day in Pickering, Ontario, John became part of the torch relay leading up to the 2010 Vancouver Winter Olympic Games. "It wasn't about me," he says. "It was about being able to touch and hold and represent what the Olympic movement is all about for a very brief moment. It was less than a mile, but to me it had the memories of a marathon."

Running a marathon, or even a mile, was definitely not part of John's lifestyle when he was a busy food industry executive. "I wasn't in very good shape," he recalls. "I was a two-pack-a-day smoker with 238 pounds on my 5'9" frame. I had neglected my own health because I threw my energy into my family, my work, and my community." One day after struggling through a fun run with his younger son, he realized he finally had to do something about his own wellness. "It was a real wake up call, so I began running. First it was just from light post to light post. Then I began to lose weight, and soon I quit smoking. Next thing I knew I was entering the local charity runs and doing reasonably well." In 1984, John decided to leave the food industry and fill a niche in the marketplace for a store where runners could purchase quality running shoes from knowledgeable and supportive salespeople, the type of store that would especially benefit beginning runners. That first small storeroom has since expanded to more than one hundred stores across Canada.

When John received the phone call to participate in the torch relay, "It came out of nowhere," he says. "They told me I had introduced so many people to running through my running store clinics that I should be one of the Olympic torch bearers." Indeed, John is well-known in Canada as an advocate for running and fitness. He has received the Award of Excellence in health promotion from the Canadian Medical Association, and was named as one of ten Canadians who are making a difference for his significant contribution to health through fitness. One of his most popular training and racing concepts from those clinics is the 10:1 program, which specifies a minute of walking for every ten minutes of running.

"Based on my schedule, we settled on a suburb of Toronto called Pickering along the route of the relay," he says. "It was going to be at 7:00 in the morning in December in this sleepy bedroom community and I thought, who's going to be there?" So when his wife asked if she should join him for the event, John told her it wouldn't be worth her trouble. "I arrived there and the torch bearers were given silvery-white tracksuits and our own torches that we were allowed to keep. The rule was that we had to maintain custody of that torch at all times because there is always the risk of someone trying to grab it as had happened in past Olympic torch relays." Just in case, there is always a backup already-lit torch kept in reserve. And for security, six Royal Canadian Mounted Police would follow the runners some distance behind wearing dark track suits to blend in. "I stepped on the bus and there were all these famous Canadian Olympians and dignitaries and politicians, and I thought, 'This is really cool!' From inside the bus I began to see all this traffic and I looked out on the streets, and they were lined with people. Then it dawned on me that this was a big deal. Next thing I knew it was my turn to run. "I got off the bus, held out my torch, and the torch bearer who ran before me lit it. I turned to start running and the crowd was cheering and people were taking pictures. There were old people from a nursing home and young children who were let out of school and families and people who stepped out of the coffee shops to watch. People who knew me were calling out my name, and even if they didn't know me they had programs that indicated who was running.

"But it wasn't about me. It was about being part of the flame that was going by. They were staring at the flame and saying, 'There's the flame! The flame's coming!' The mesmerizing effect it had on people was overwhelming. I've seen it before on TV, but you don't realize the emotion when it passes by unless you are there. So I told myself to slow down and savor it because it wasn't going to be very long. But soon I realized it was more than just the Canadian torch run; it was being seen around the world, and at that moment the magnitude of it hit me and I became quite emotional. After all, this was the flame from Athens and I was getting to hold it!

"All of a sudden I could see the people but I couldn't hear them anymore; it all became quiet. I thought, this is what it's all about. This is what athletes have competed for all these years. I'm carrying that symbol of athleticism. I'm representing all those people and what they had accomplished as well as those who will be competing in upcoming Olympic Games. What a powerful and inspiring moment it was!

"Next thing I knew I'm at the exchange point and I touched torches with the next runner and they extinguished mine. But that wasn't the end because they took some of us to city hall where there were more festivities. And there it was like I was a rock star. People crowded around me and wanted to get a picture of me with the flame, and everybody wanted to touch it—kids, old people, professional people, street people. The crowd was so thick around me that the organizers had to take me out of the crowd and get me back onto the stage. Later, back home when I explained it all to my wife, she said, 'But you told me it was going to be just another race!'

"Just remembering it now brings back that same feeling that is so very unique and special. We all remember our first run and our first marathon, and before the torch relay the Ironman World Championship in Hawaii was the highlight of my running career. But this was more than a personal accomplishment. It was about the magnitude of everything that is athletic, everything that is good. When you see something as simple as the flame going by and how it can unite and empower the community in such a special way, to me that is what the Olympic movement is all about."

Running Tip: "Don't see the race as a test but as a celebration. When we experience being in an organized race we discover a sense of community, and the sense of community we get from running is so powerful. Cheer, encourage, and inspire others in your race and you will be inspired too."

Zola Budd Pieterse

Some runners are motivated to cross the finish line first for the medal that is draped around their neck. Some are spurred on to greatness by the fame that typically follows. And others seek the top spot on the podium for the prize money awarded the victor. But a little barefoot girl in South Africa was racing for something completely different. She cared little about a medal, was not seeking notoriety, and knew no check would arrive in her bank account if she were triumphant. Zola Budd wanted to win her race for one thing and one thing only: a red duffel bag.

"I always knew I could run fast even before going to school," she recalls. "I could beat my older cousins in all the running games we played. They could never catch me, so I knew I was faster than most kids. At school I was really bad at swimming and gymnastics and any ball sports, but running just came naturally to me; it was easy compared to everything else."

Zola began running seriously at age twelve, and catapulted onto the world stage five years later at the 1984 Olympics (running for Great Britain) where she famously tangled with Mary Decker Slaney in the 3,000-meter final. Even before that race she was known as the girl who competed barefoot, an oddity to most observers around the world. "For me it was strange that other people thought *I* was strange for running barefoot," she recalls. "Growing up in South Africa, most kids run barefoot. For us it was a natural way of life. Even today at the primary and elementary school level, students who run and play organized sports are not allowed to wear shoes. We think it's healthier for them, that it's better for the child's development to go barefoot.

When you take your kids to the pediatrician for the first time, you're told to keep your kids barefoot for as long as possible."

In 1981 with only two years of serious training, Zola was generating excitement in South Africa not for her bare feet but for her performances at the junior level. The South African Junior Track Championships would be Zola's first big national meet, and she had been entered in the 1,500-meter run. "I was fourteen and it was the first big event I had ever competed in, and it was also in my hometown of Bloemfontein," she says. After she finished second in that race, she decided to run the shorter 800-meter distance the next day, just for the experience. "I was just going to do it and enjoy it," she says of the two-lap race in which she would not be one of the favorites. But possibly there was more incentive for her entering that race than just the opportunity to gain competitive experience and to "enjoy it." As she recalls, "After coming in second the previous evening in the 1,500, I remember that when they gave out the medals for all the races, they played this trumpet theme and each winner got this red gym bag. It was amazing to me that you could actually win that! I'd missed out on it."

The fourteen-year-old who was so easily impressed with a red bag was not easily intimidated in her 800-meter race, possibly because the expectations were so low. "One of the reasons the race was so special was that no one expected me to win. There was a girl who could run fifty-four seconds for the 400 meters, and she was obviously the favorite. At the start, to be honest, I was so relaxed and wasn't worried about anything. I just went to the front and stayed there and kept waiting for the others to pass me. They stayed with me until the last hundred meters and I kept waiting for that one girl to pass because I knew she was coming." Admittedly, Zola remembers little about the specifics of that race except for the bag waiting for her at the finish. "The favorite never got past me. I was coming down the final straight and I was outsprinting her and at sixty meters I was thinking, 'I'm going to win that red bag! I'm going to win that red bag!' That's the only thing that went through my mind.

"My parents were there at the finish," she says, "and I

remember getting on the winning podium with my red bag. I got a medal too but (she laughs) that wasn't as important as my bag. That race changed my whole running career because it was my first big championship title and it gave me the confidence to carry on from there. After that race I started believing a bit more in myself and got a bit more confidence in my running. I look back on that race especially when I see young girls out running and racing and I think how one race can change a whole career."

Three years later Zola Budd set a world record in the 5,000-meter run. But world records are meant to be broken; a red duffel bag is forever. "I still have that bag," she says proudly. "It's my most precious possession."

Running Tip: "You don't always have to go out looking to make a race memorable; sometimes it just happens when you least expect it. It's more on a subconscious level that it happens—just a moment in time."

Scott Tinley

Mike F

The Hawaii Ironman Triathlon, now known as the Ironman World Championship, derived from the concept of combining the three toughest endurance races in Hawaii—the 2.4-mile Waikiki Roughwater Swim, the 112-mile Around-Oahu Bike Race, and the 26.2-mile Honolulu Marathon—into one event. In 1981, the year Scott Tinley first entered, the race moved from Waikiki to the lava fields of the Kona Coast on the Big Island of Hawaii, where athletes have to complete the 140.6-mile journey under scorching sun, and through blistering heat and severe crosswinds. "In 1981 there was nothing at stake," says Scott. "There was no sponsorship, no prize money, and I had zero expectations. I didn't care where I placed. I just wanted to finish the damn thing."

Scott was a frustrated athlete growing up in San Diego, something he believes eventually steered him to long distance events in which he could compete alone. "I had one of those childhoods where I struggled to find real social acceptance and connection in the youth team sports area," he says. "I just wasn't that good in baseball, basketball, football, and soccer, and that is often the impetus for elite athletes and a connection with individual endurance sports." But Scott's abilities in a wide variety of fitness-related pursuits leant themselves to success in a new sport called the triathlon, which was first documented in his California community in the mid 1970s. He recalls that many of those early triathletes were either brilliant swimmers, great bikers, or fantastic runners, but that their skill in the other two disciplines was lacking, enabling those with competence in all three areas to fare much better. "I was a Jack of all trades," he recalls, "with average skills honed over a lifestyle of living on the beach, lifeguarding, learning how to swim, riding my bike, and running in high school. Suddenly I'm a triathlete. To finish a race in the top ten with a borrowed beach cruiser bike, my surf trunks, and running shoes that only *looked* like running shoes wasn't bad. All those failings like getting kicked off the football team, not making the baseball team, being too short for the basketball team—well, now I could go back to my tenth high school reunion and say 'I'm pretty good at something.'"

As the sport evolved those first few years, it was more of a learn-as-you-go mentality with respect to training, racing, fueling, and appropriate gear. "In the late seventies and early eighties there was no playbook," says Scott. "Nobody really had any idea how one was to prepare for a multiple sport event, let alone one that took all day." Indeed, most triathlons at the time lasted less than ninety minutes. The inaugural Hawaii Ironman race in 1978 was the first long distance event staged in the swim/bike/run format. As Scott recalls, "All of us felt like lab rats. The things that we did were completely ridiculous without basis in physiological fact. It's very laughable now. From a lifestyle standpoint I backed into it. I was working ten days a month as a firefighter and had twenty days off each month, so I thought why not take a year to focus on training and see what I could do? Soon each week I was riding four hundred miles, running ninety to a hundred, and swimming fifty thousand yards. I was always tired, always beat up, always sore, but I was incredibly happy. And I thought, 'All right, this doesn't suck.'"

It wasn't until a feature about 1979 Ironman winner Tom Warren appeared in *Sports Illustrated* that the rest of the nation began to take notice of the nascent sport. "Tom lived down the street and gave me the article to read," Scott recalls. "He said I should think about doing it, and I committed myself to the '81 race. 1981 was the first year the event was held in its present location on the Big Island. It was also the first time TV coverage was planned and advertised in advance; it wasn't some accidental thing like what happened the year before when there was a little TV time left over from a golf tournament. It was the first time for many things in that event.

"The only training notebook I had was talking to guys like Tom Warren, guys who could make a decent living and still have heaps of time off to train. In hindsight it seems humorous to think how naïve we were in terms of things like aerodynamics. I wanted to keep cool so I wore a tank top and let the wind blow through my shirt. I didn't want my feet to hurt on the bike so I wore tennis shoes instead of cycling shoes. And we didn't understand the dynamics of weight. I rode with a tool kit on my bike that weighed five pounds. I could have built a '67 VW with the stuff in that kit!" Scott had enough money for the flight to Hawaii for himself and his wife, but not much for anything else. "Back then you could have certain outside support, but I couldn't afford a rental car so my wife had to sit back in town." With no support, no expectations, and little knowledge of aerodynamics and the effects of added weight, Scott started the race.

"In the swim, I knew I'd get beat on the head a little at the start, but I could go off to the side and take it easy," he says. "My swim wasn't fast but it wasn't terrible. But on the bike I kept expecting something bad to happen. I was concerned that I didn't have a map of the course, and when I asked an official he said that there's only one left turn and then you come back. I remember during the race I looked over at another competitor who had a large glass jar of peanut butter duct taped to his handlebar where he could dip his fingers in it. I thought, 'That guy's so smart, I'll never be like him.'" Unlike the five thousand dollar carbon fiber racing bikes of today, Scott's bike was the economy model. "I bought my bike when I was a firefighter/paramedic for $189. It wasn't high tech by any means, but it did have ten gears."

Despite incurring one flat tire, Scott made fairly good progress along the Queen Ka'ahumanu Highway through the barren landscape of black lava rocks. Soon, however, he realized an important element that his low tech ten-speed bike lacked: a comfy seat. "I don't remember too much about that ride," he says, "but I do remember how uncomfortable my butt was. It was my first really long ride. I remember thinking that I just couldn't wait to get off the bike and start the marathon. How ironic was that? I was coasting along in the breeze and I couldn't wait to start a 26.2-mile run in 90-degree heat and 85% humidity because my ass hurt."

Running was Scott's strength. He had previously run a 2:30 marathon on very little training and without any coaching. Of course, there hadn't been a 2.4-mile swim and 112-mile bike ride leading up to it. "For the run I had no expectations except that I might have to walk a little bit," he recalls. "But I didn't walk at all while a lot of people did. Perhaps it was something compassionate in me, but when I went by somebody who was walking, I felt compelled to stop and talk to them and ask how they were doing. I did that a couple of times but then thought that if I did that with everyone in front of me I'd never finish. When I got off the bike, I was barely in the top fifty, but somehow I eventually passed between forty and forty-five runners. To do that I used that notion of immediate gratification, or as my friends called it, Pac-Man syndrome; every person you pass feeds you a little bit of energy. I went from forty-sixth off the bike and suddenly I was in the top ten. Then I caught number nine, then eight, then seven …. My marathon time off the bike wasn't fast, maybe I ran a 3:22. But everybody else was running 3:45 to 4:15, so you could make up gobs of time back then. I think I passed the third-place guy with about a half mile to go."

Unlike the atmosphere at the finish line of today's Ironman World Championship—thousands of sun-drenched fans, the splash of logos and sponsors' banners, the global media presence—Scott was met by thirty or forty curious onlookers and one camera crew. Nevertheless, he knew he had accomplished something special that day. "It was unadulterated joy," he recalls. "Third place was as good as winning. The visceral feeling of success was so powerful because I had no expectations. I was a kid fresh out of college working with a couple of different career choices and had finished third best in an emerging sport that a lot of people were beginning to look at really closely."

Scott Tinley would go on to win the 1982 and 1985 Ironman World Championship, become a three-time winner of the

Ironman World Series, and be inducted into both the Triathlon and Ironman Hall of Fame upon his retirement in 1999. But the 1981 Ironman is the one race he keeps coming back to. It was a time of innocence in the sport and in his career as an athlete, and a time he knew could never be recaptured. "There was no commercial aspect to it in terms of remuneration," he says. "There was no notion of 'If I do this I will get this,' and no thought of how one might take this achievement and transpose it into something of value. But you could feel it, and you could sense that this thing wasn't going to go away.

"After that '81 race it all changed. Because of the TV coverage, the entries doubled to about seven hundred the following year. In '81 I had absolute anonymity and everything after that came with a burden of expectations. Reporters started calling me and I became conflicted. How do I handle all this? I think for the most part I erred on the side of not letting it upset my morality and spirituality and my commitment to what the sport meant to me. It was an important event for me for what it signified and what it created and how it reminded me of how far I'd come. And when I look back on that event now I think how innocent, how naive, and how pure it was in so many ways. That's why I think about that race as a powerful and enjoyable moment in my life."

Running Tip: "Do it for yourself and not for your sponsors, fans, media, or your family. I've seen so many examples where athletes become frustrated because they thought they had failed; somehow the results didn't meet their standards because their motivations were more extrinsic than intrinsic."

Amy Hastings

You think you've felt pressure? Sure, entering a race with hopes of running fast enough to qualify for the Boston Marathon can be a bit stressful. Nevertheless, whether you hit the wall and fail, or run well and achieve your desired time, life goes on. Come Monday you return to your job with another race under your belt and an interesting story to tell your coworkers. But what if running *is* your job? And what if your performance in a particular race determines whether you continue to live the life of a professional runner or lose your sponsorship and means of financial support, effectively ending your running career? Now *that's* pressure.

"All I had was running. I was committing 100% of my life to it and it wasn't going well." Unlike most of us, Amy Hastings is among the select few elite runners who make a living from track and road racing. Along with a running-shoe contract that provides a base salary, there is prize money, performance bonuses, and appearance fees that enable them to hire top-notch coaches, travel to racing venues around the world, and train full-time without the stress and time commitment of a nine-to-five job. That is, until their performance declines and sponsors pull their shoe contracts. "Through college and just after graduation I saw steady improvement in my running," says Amy. "When I went pro, things didn't go as well for me for a really long time. There were so many ups and downs and running wasn't as fun as it had been." Amy had originally run for Adidas, but when her performance was not up to the sponsor's standards, the contract was not renewed. "I knew I could keep working at it and make something happen. I just wanted a sponsor to give me a chance.

I was running terribly at the time, and it would be a real long shot that anyone would give me anything, so I was really lucky when Brooks decided to pick me up." Given a second chance, Amy had to perform well in races to give Brooks the desired exposure. Otherwise the shoe company could decide to let her go and find the next up-and-coming runner to promote their product.

At about the same time, Amy changed the focus of her running to the marathon distance, after being known throughout her career as a 5,000- and 10,000-meter runner. "Back in high school if you asked me what my best event would eventually be, I would say the marathon. Sunday long runs were what I enjoyed more than anything else in my training," she says, "so running the marathon was something I had wanted to do for a long time." But training to compete at a new distance was a gamble, especially with her career languishing and a new sponsor impatient for results. "Brooks had picked me up, but I wasn't getting them any return at that point. It felt like I had just been banging my head against the wall for a long time." Fortunately for Amy, the decision to leave the track and take to the road was the impetus that jump-started her stalled career. "It's funny," she recalls, "but when I began training it felt like the marathon was what I was built for, what I was meant to do. I started enjoying running again.

"My 5K and 10K training was more intense, but for the marathon my emphasis was on the long runs to get my mileage up. Those kinds of runs just make me feel stronger, and I just enjoy them. I run how I feel; I don't worry about my time." Along with a secondary focus on tempo runs, Amy boosted her weekly mileage past the century mark. A minor Achilles injury kept her out of the Houston Marathon, so Amy set her sights on the March 2011 Los Angeles Marathon. "I really had to make something happen in LA," she says, "not only to prove it to the shoe companies but to prove it to myself too. So there was definitely a lot of pressure on me for this race. It was getting to the point where it was make-or-break with my sponsorship contracts. I wouldn't have been able to continue very much longer. Up to that point I had lived this dream that I could one day be an Olympian. It was starting to become more of a reality that it was *not* going to happen. There was still that little bit of a spark and I was trying just to keep that alive, but I was starting to think that maybe I had just been crazy all those years."

Like anyone does before a big race, Amy went through a mix of emotions at the starting line in Los Angeles. "That morning it was like my first race again," she recalls. "I hadn't been that excited in years, and I was dead set on doing it the best as I possibly could. It was a brand new distance and I had always loved the long distances, but at the same time I was terrified because the longest run I had done up to then was twenty-four miles. What if I got to 24.1 and completely exploded? It was unknown territory for me, so it was scary but really exciting. I had heard all these horror stories from people, so I was just going to try and expect the unexpected."

Something that was unexpected was the bad weather, but according to Amy, that was a good thing. "The best thing that happened was that the weather was so terrible. It was so windy that the mile markers along the course had blown over. I would be getting random splits but nothing made sense." Without knowing where she was on the course, she went back to the way she ran her long training runs: running by feel and not worrying about the clock. "I just went internal and ran how I felt. It's a great experience when you can run just by feel and not by time." Something else that took her mind off of her time was a strong rain that engulfed the runners soon after the start. "There was this torrential downpour coming in off the coast that we got stuck in. We hit it about a third of the way into the race but it didn't even affect me. I was prepared for it and I loved it.

"The only point on the course I knew for sure was the halfway mark when I saw 13.1. I looked down at my watch and it was a lot faster than I really wanted to run. I think if I had known my split times earlier I would have forced myself to slow down, but I felt so good and it wasn't scary for me. At that point I had stopped caring about all the pressure on me before the race and was focused on getting to the finish line as fast as I could.

I just wanted to do it for me. It was an incredible experience."

Through the wind and the rain, Amy and two other women, Ethiopians Buzunesh Deba and Mare Dibaba, had pulled away from the rest of the female runners in the race. They kept within sight of each other, and Amy actually held a short lead going into mile twenty. "Everyone tells you that you really begin to feel it at mile twenty," she says about running a marathon. "At mile nineteen I was thinking that I might be able to win this thing since I felt so good. But at mile twenty there was such a quick change in how I felt. It just became painful very quickly because my muscles were running out of glycogen. The pain was over my entire body—an achy feeling everywhere. You immediately want to slow down, and I did. But then I tried to run a little faster and it didn't hurt any worse, so I was able to pick up the pace again. The thing about the LA Marathon is that two or three of the last six miles are downhill, so that was a big help." By then the other two women had gone ahead, but Amy threw in a surge and caught them. "With three miles to go Mare dropped back but then Deba took off, and there was nothing I could do at that point to catch her." Amy fought through the pain to hold her place and finish second in a time of 2:27:03, making her the eighth-best American women's marathoner of all time.

Of course, considering that Amy's future as a professional runner depended on that result, second place was as good as a win. "It invigorated me," she recalls. "I was so excited after that because it went so well and there wasn't as much pressure on me anymore." Another consequence of her race and her marathon training was the mileage base she had in place for upcoming races on the rack. "I was excited to get back on the track and see how I could do. Running the longer distances in training made me stronger in the shorter distances and really helped me." Indeed, after a disappointing fourth-place finish in the 2012 Olympic Trials marathon in only her second race at that distance, Amy focused on running the 10K trials later that summer. "I really wanted to compete in the marathon, but I figured more than anything I wanted to be an Olympian," she says.

Amy realized her dream of becoming an Olympian by

winning the 10,000 meters at the trials, something she agrees would not have been possible without her performance in LA. "The LA Marathon was the reason I was able to continue running competitively," she says. "If it wasn't for LA, I would have had to get a normal job because at some point you have to look at where your finances are. But no matter what I do in the future, I don't think I'll ever stop running. Going for a morning run will always be a part of my life. Even when it was a struggle I loved just getting out there and running. It helps me think. It's good for everything."

Running Tip: "A lot of times your best races will come after your toughest times, both physical and emotional. So just get through it, and keep working. It's the people who can get through that and bounce back that end up having their best races and breakthrough performances."

Chris Russell

When talking to Chris Russell about his best race, one is reminded of the old Remington TV commercial in which the spokesman says, "I liked the shaver so much, I bought the company." In Chris's case, he liked the race so much, he became the race director. But his leap from novice road runner to head honcho of the Groton, Massachusetts 10K road race took many years and many miles to become reality. And if it wasn't for wrestling, it may never have happened at all.

"I was terrible at any sport that required any kind of hand-eye coordination," says Chris. "I was always the kid that got stuck in right field who they hoped nobody would hit the ball to." But when the athletically challenged youth enrolled in high school, he was forced to choose a competitive sport as part of the curriculum. "The sport I ended up in was wrestling," he says. "It is an individual sport and has less to do with hand-eye coordination and more to do with training and strength and pain tolerance." Chris soon learned that the entire wrestling squad also ran on the cross-country team to get in shape, and that became his introduction to competitive running. "I liked it, though I was always a midpacker," he recalls. "I would finish somewhere around 125 out of the 300+ field, but I learned the basics of training and pacing and racing."

The lessons he learned from wrestling and cross-country, however, were put aside as college, then a job, a family, and frequent business travel competed for his time in the ensuing years. Eventually, at age twenty-nine and at a weight of 220 pounds, Chris realized he was out of shape, overweight, and needed to do something about it. "I remembered how to run from high school, but I had no fitness," he recalls. "I started running with a guy at work and we got up to five miles every other day at lunch, and I just fell in love with it. Not just the physical aspect of running but the mental aspect of it. The way it just freed up my mind and let my creativity flow, it just seemed so worthy.

"Then one day my mother called and said they were starting a new road race in Groton, which is where I grew up, so now I had something to train for. This was sort of my rebirth into running," he remembers fondly. "It was a 10K, which actually was a really long distance for me at that point. That spring I began training for the race and started throwing in some long runs on the weekends. I ran an eight miler as my long run to prepare for the race because my goal pace was to be under eight minutes per mile. It doesn't sound like much, but at the time I was out of shape and heavy and didn't know how fast I could go."

To clear up some of that uncertainty, Chris did a test run of the course the weekend before the race, but it did not have the intended result. "I had been in California on business and flew back sleep deprived and jet-lagged," he recalls. "I went out to do the test run and at one point I had to stop and walk. I couldn't break my eight-minute-per-mile time and I was just totally depressed. So that whole week I was miserable. I was so hard to live with and I was snapping at everyone because I knew my first race was going to kick my ass."

Not surprisingly, Chris was anxious at the starting line on race day. "I was nervous as hell," he recalls. Standing in the crowd, I was miserable because I had no idea what to expect." Seeking any advantage he could, Chris had visited the course again the day before and marked off every quarter mile for the first two miles. "By memorizing the location of each mark and the split that I needed to be on that mark, I was able to keep my pace under control for the first two miles and avoid going out too fast." From his high school racing, Chris knew how to draft behind people and how to run hills, which helped him on the rolling New England course. But the key for him was holding his pace for as long as he could, especially when the course turned into a headwind. "I didn't mark all the course, so the only way I knew whether or not I was on track was at the mile marks," he says. "I had to hit the mile marks and do the math. I kept focusing on maintaining that pace and trying to relax into the effort and into the pain.

"I was so convinced that I was going to do horribly that when I reached five miles it all started to become amazing to me," he says. "I was running between 7:40 and 7:50 pace, and the fact that I wasn't doing horribly was a total surprise and a revelation. But there was still this dramatic tension. I was doing well, but the other shoe could always drop because I felt I was on borrowed time once I got to those later miles. I was doing well but I still felt that the good feeling could end any second. It wasn't until I crossed the six-mile mark and could see the track where the finish line was that I realized I was going to make my goal; I was going to run under eight-minutes-per-mile pace. Right then my daughter, who at the time would have been one or two years old, stepped out of the crowd, leaned into the course, and gave me a high five. I clearly remember—and I'm tearing up saying this—I clearly remember the emotional hit of running at that 7:40 pace and beating my goal in my first 10K and having my family there. It was just … it was something I'll never forget."

According to Chris, finishing the race "was like no other feeling in the world, a feeling of accomplishment and euphoria. Whether it's a thirty-year-old running the 10K to get back in shape or some kid running the children's 2K, a race like this can be a catalyst for someone else like me to be reborn in our sport, and that is one of the reasons I wanted to be race director. Four years ago the race got in trouble when the race director couldn't do it anymore, so I stepped in and made the phone calls, got a team together, and got the race back on track. Maybe you can't quantify it, but everyone knows how important this is to the community. And not just for the runners. It's important to have this opportunity for families to come together and celebrate springtime and a healthy lifestyle. We have to do that. When it was in trouble a few years back I wasn't willing to let that die."

Since then, the author of *The Mid-Packer's Lament* has run twenty-two Groton Road Races, more than thirty marathons, and has fully embraced the runner's life. "I come up with my best ideas when I'm running," he says. "You're just incredibly lucid where your brain is being bathed in those happy running chemicals. And looking back, it was that first race which was the keystone for all of this."

Running Tip: "You have to take a step back and take the long view of your training. I see runners all the time training for the marathon and getting injured. They ask how they can still keep on training for the event, but they should really be asking how they can keep training for life. Running is part of a longer time frame. If you miss a year because of injury, eventually it will heal and you'll be back to doing what you love. I can't always be faster, and I can't always run longer, but I can always enjoy it. Sure, you can be competitive, but you have to do it in such a way that you don't sacrifice the gift."

Trisha Meili

Trisha Meili crosses the finish line in the 2003 Hope & Possibility Run

During a run through Central Park on the night of April 19, 1989, Trisha Meili was attacked, raped, beaten beyond recognition, and left for dead. "I went for a run and had my life interrupted," she writes in her best-selling memoir. The Wall Street investment banker suffered traumatic brain injury, lost nearly eighty percent of her blood, remained in a coma for two weeks, and spent the next month in a state of delirium. Doctors predicted she would never regain her physical or mental capabilities.

Fourteen years after that incident gripped the nation, Trisha went public with her story in *I Am the Central Park Jogger: A Story of Hope and Possibility*. It is a book about courage and the capacity of the human body and spirit to heal. It is also about the gift of hope that sustained her through months of rehabilitation and remains with her in the never-ending process of recovery. Like the writing of her book, Trisha's best race also came fourteen years after the attack. But just as she had to relearn how to talk, tell time, feed herself, and button her blouse, she also had to relearn how to walk and run before even thinking about racing again. Her first attempt at running came five months after the attack.

"I wasn't a fabulous runner," she says, "I was pretty average with my times, but it was the sport of running that I loved, just to be outside and in nature." Trisha even had a few marathons to her credit, but after the attack she realized she would never be able to run at the same level as before. "I hoped that I could run and be able to enjoy being outdoors like I used to, but I had this inner knowledge or wisdom that it's not going to be the same. When the time came to run again, I was just going to take it easy." The time for that first run, however, came much sooner than she expected. "I had just gotten out of the wheelchair and started to walk again without assistance," she recalls, when she received an invitation from Nelson Carvalho, the head of the Physical Therapy department at Gaylord Hospital in Connecticut. "When he casually mentioned there was a group of people meeting on weekends at the hospital to run and asked if I wanted to join them, I remember thinking to myself, 'Are you nuts?' I think I was a little frightened. Am I ready for this? Is it too soon?"

Nevertheless, Trisha's trust in Nelson eventually convinced her that it was not too soon. "In rehab you're so vulnerable and you want to feel safe and you don't want to hurt yourself," she says. "But I trusted him. He was gently persistent and I thought that if he's going to be there it will be okay." A few weeks later she joined several others on the quarter-mile loop that went around and through the parking lot of the rehab hospital. "There were four or five others there," she recalls. "There was one guy in a wheelchair and a couple on crutches and one guy with spina bifida. It really motivated me to think that if they were going to do this with the challenges they had, then I can give it a try and see what happens.

"Nelson stayed with me as we started out and I remember that I was barely moving. I was wobbling … *but I was doing it!* Nelson wasn't holding me, and that was the beauty of it. It was different than in my physical therapy sessions when you're one-on-one with the therapist and she says to do this or that; this was so much freer. It was like, okay, I see where I'm supposed to go so let's try this. Even though I was stumbling a little bit, it just felt so good, like I had just conquered the world. It was a huge achievement for me. The freedom of being outside and being able to have that feeling of running again just filled me with such joy and hope. I probably wasn't thinking about it right then, but afterwards I remember what made it so powerful was that I was taking something back that had been taken away from me.

"At some point near the end of the run I thought about going around for another lap. With rehab you come to realize that you have to push yourself and that's how you move forward. So I thought about going around again, but then I remember thinking that, no, that was enough, I'll just stop here and feel really good about myself. And in some ways I just felt proud of myself for being able to recognize that. That I could feel I didn't have to go around gain until I got stronger and that it was okay to stop. So, it was just a spectacular morning for me."

Trisha learned that the other participants at those Gaylord weekend runs were members of an Achilles Track Club chapter (now known as Achilles International), the nonprofit whose mission is to encourage people with disabilities to participate in a running program to promote personal achievement and self-esteem. "Seeing those other people with their challenges and disabilities has always stuck with me," says Trisha. "I felt a deep bond with them." Years later when she was contacted by the founder of Achilles International, Dick Traum, Trisha was strong enough to volunteer at the Saturday morning workouts at the New York City chapter. "I wanted to volunteer because I realized how much that first run did for me," she says. "In my rehab, the confidence I gained in reaching a physical goal could be transferred to other aspects of my life, and for me that's what

Achilles International is all about." Soon Trisha joined the board of Achilles International and became the catalyst for organizing a road race for Achilles athletes.

It was in 2002 when the nonprofit received permission from New York Road Runners to hold a 5-mile run in Central Park, and the first race was in June of the following year. "It was such a good feeling to be able to bring a sense of achievement to people with disabilities. There are other races that people with disabilities participate in, but this was a race that was sponsored *by* people with disabilities, inviting the able-bodied to join us. It was our race, people with disabilities own it. The spirit in Central Park the morning of the race was like nothing I ever experienced before," she recalls. "We had about two hundred entered. There was just so much excitement and gratitude because people were thankful that they were being allowed to participate no matter what challenges they had. And you could just see it with the smiles on all the faces. It was very powerful."

As an Achilles International volunteer, Trisha was experienced guiding physically impaired runners during their regular Saturday morning workouts. But never before had she guided a *visually* impaired runner as she would do in this race, nor someone who was also a well-known political figure. "I was nervous because I hadn't guided anyone who was visually impaired before," she says, "and he was a pretty senior politician in government. But we shared this bond of each having challenges even though they were different challenges." The runner Trisha guided that day was David Paterson, who was serving in the New York State Senate at the time. Five years later he would be sworn in as the fifty-fifth governor of New York. "David is not totally without sight, but still I was nervous, and we didn't have a tether to keep us together. He said to just let him know what's coming and what's around, so as we were going I would tell him the landmarks we were passing, which mile marker we reached, and when we were about to go up or down a hill. It was fun and he runs fast, so it was a challenge for both of us."

The course also presented a challenge to Trisha of a

different kind, one not related to hills, or speed, or the guiding of a disabled runner. "The route goes by where I was attacked," she says, "and I was conscious of it as we ran by, but it made me realize how grateful I was that I had recovered as much as I had. I also felt proud of the hard work that got me to the point where I could run right by there." As Trisha discussed in her book, one of the lessons she learned in recovery is how critical it is to pour one's energy into the present rather than be preoccupied with the past.

"The race started on the east side of the park for that first year and the finish was on a downhill. David tells me now that I was pushing him to go faster, and I tell him that he was pushing me, but we were both trying to go faster down that hill with the finish line in the distance. When we crossed the line I had a sense of being exhausted but I was also filled with so much joy because we did it! We gave each other a huge hug. We were sweating profusely because it was so hot, but we didn't care. It was just fabulous."

The popularity of the race has grown each year, and organizers now have to limit the field to 5,000 runners. "I've been running that race every year," says Trisha, "and each time I get a little slower. But my absolute favorite part of it is after I finish, so I can wait there to encourage people to keep pushing to the end. By the time I'm finished all the fast people are already passed, so it's good to be able to cheer on those who really need that encouragement to finish. It's a great feeling when you acknowledge someone and they just brighten up and pick up their pace. That cheering at the end makes such a difference for the runners, you see it in the smiles on everybody's face. I love to be a part of that. It's just a tremendously inspiring race."

These days Trisha Meili is a motivational speaker, encouraging people around the world to overcome life's obstacles and get back on the road to life. That is also the goal of the Hope & Possibility 5-mile Run, although that name was not the first one considered. Initially, Dick Traum of Achilles International wanted to name the race after Trisha since she was the race's founder, but Trisha declined. "I said let's call it the

Hope & Possibility Race. That term was on my mind because my own story is about hope and possibility, and in all the ways people and events happen to give me hope. When I see the runners finish, especially those with disabilities, I can feel that sense that they accomplish more than they thought they could. And that's what really captures the spirit of the race. When there's hope, possibility emerges."

Running Tip: "Feel proud of what you *can* do."

Marty Liquori

"In some of your greatest races you may be in over your head, so you just go out and run as hard as you can." That was the strategy Marty Liquori used in what he recalls fondly as the best race he ever ran. Never mind that he would soon become only the third high school runner in history to break four minutes for the mile, or that he would win a spot on the 1968 Olympic team as a college freshman, or that he would one day outkick the great Jim Ryun in the famous Dream Mile. His come-from-behind victory at the Penn Relays as the anchor on the Essex Catholic High School Distance Medley team was the real life changer. "After that race I had to reevaluate everything because it gave me the confidence that I might be something special as a runner."

Being a runner was not Marty's only passion at the time; he also loved the guitar. He even played in a band until his coach learned their gigs sometimes fell on the nights before Marty's races. "My coach visited my parents and told them I should concentrate on running," he says, and even Marty concedes he had more talent on the track than on the stage. So, with guitar playing on hold, Marty sharpened his speed with regular interval workouts of 12 x 400 at 60 seconds, and bolstered his endurance with 15-mile long runs every other week, leading up to the Penn Relays.

"One thing about the Penn Relays I remember," says Marty, "is that you're in a sport where you run in front of fifty people for ninety percent of your life and then one day you have thirty thousand people in the stands yelling; it's a totally different experience." Known officially as the Penn Relay Carnival, the three-day celebration of track and field in Philadelphia has hosted more athletes than any other single meet in the world. While many individual events are contested, it is the college and high school relays that create the most excitement each year. The distance medley involves a relay of a half mile, quarter mile, three-quarters of a mile, and then a mile, in that order. "It wasn't like a regular race because we don't all start together," says Marty. Indeed, once he received the baton for his anchor leg, the race leader had a 60-yard advantage. "I was just running as fast as I could, chasing this guy who was way out in front."

A key to Marty's performance that day was never knowing how fast he was actually running, which otherwise might have caused him to run more conservatively for fear of fading at the end. "Since the meet is so early in the season, I had no indication of how fast I would be able to run," he says, "and the Tartan track surface was throwing off all my perceptions because I was used to running on a dirt track." But keeping Marty in the dark about his pace was something his coach had planned all along. As Marty recalls, "I didn't know what I ran the first quarter mile in, but it was probably something like fifty-eight seconds. If the people in the stands knew I had just run a 58-second lap, they would have thought I was either going to die out there or else run quite a race. But my coach, knowing it would freak me out to be running that fast for the first lap, yelled 'sixty-two.' Then I came around again after the half mile and I was probably at two minutes, and he yelled '2:04.' Eventually I ended up catching the guy, and we set a national record that stood for many years. After the race my coach admitted he was lying about the times so I wouldn't cut back on my speed." Marty's time of 4:04 for that mile beat his personal best by an astonishing nine seconds. "I was pretty shocked," he says. "That's the great thing about running. Only three or four years before that I was amazed anyone could run under five minutes. You go from being a 5-minute miler to 4:04 in the space of a couple of years and the lesson it should teach you is to never underestimate yourself. It's within all of us."

Up until then the 4:13 miler had aspirations of attending

an Ivy League school primarily for the education; running would just be the means for him to remain on scholarship while preparing for a career on Wall Street. But his 4:04 time at the Penn Relays turned the heads of college coaches and convinced him he could compete with the best. "My coach told me I had a special talent and that maybe I should follow that talent. When the recruiters visited from the University of Pennsylvania, they said I could be the first 4-minute miler ever in the Ivy League, but after my race I realized I'd be pretty bored if I'm already the best guy coming in as a freshman. Then Jumbo Elliot of Villanova, the best coach on the east coach and maybe in the country, told me that if I went to his school I would only be the fifth fastest guy on the team. He said there would be four other guys beating me and pushing me in practice every day.

"So that was the decision I had to make. Did I want to be a big fish in a small pond, or did I want to be a small fish in a big pond and fight my way up?" Marty became a small fish, and the friendly competition with his Villanova teammates molded him into a champion who would eventually be inducted into the Track and Field Hall of Fame. "At Villanova I had four guys who had broken the four-minute mile to train with. I made the Olympic team in the 1,500 meters as a freshman, and that would only have happened if I was training with guys at that level." Marty would go on to win three straight NCAA one-mile titles, nine Penn Relays titles, and a total of fourteen national titles. Injuries kept him out of subsequent Olympic Games, but before retiring he would hold the world number one ranking in both the mile and the 5,000 meters.

Once his competitive running career was over, Marty put the same intensity into his new ventures as he had in his training and racing. He became cofounder of the Athletic Attic chain of running stores, an author, a commentator for the ABC and NBC Olympics broadcasts, and a spokesperson for the Leukemia and Lymphoma Society's Team in Training, an organization that has trained over half a million runners and raised over $1.3 billion to fund lifesaving research. "The good thing about sport is you do it in one aspect of your life, then you move on to the next aspect of your life and you realize you can also be successful in that new area. It just takes a lot of hard work." A case in point is his current stint as a musician. Without a coach looking over his shoulder and with more time to practice, Marty did something he hadn't done since high school; he picked up his guitar. Now, he and his jazz band can be heard two nights a week at a popular Gainesville, Florida restaurant.

When Marty Liquori looks back on the Penn Relays distance medley, he cannot help but think of the influence that 4:04 mile had on his life. "It was a pretty bold thing to do," he says, referring to his decision to try and become the best runner he could be at Villanova rather than pursue an Ivy League degree and a career on Wall Street, "but it happened to turn out well for me." Entrepreneur, author, commentator, fund-raiser. It seems that in running, business, or on stage with his guitar, Marty Liquori always knew the right chords.

Running Tip: "It's all in the preparation. You have to be consistent in your training and sometimes that takes years. But then you'll have the platform from which to launch your best race ever. There's no secret, it's just hard work."

Craig Virgin

Craig Virgin winning the 1980 World Cross-Country Championship

If you listen to the BBC broadcast of the 1980 World Cross-Country Championship, you would think Great Britain's Nick Rose was on his way to certain victory.

"Nick Rose is doing it in style. Half a mile to go and the challenge is vanishing. And the English that are here in the stands have gone down to the side of the track to cheer him on. This could be one of the great victories."

It was indeed a great victory, but not for Nick Rose; the last half mile was his undoing. The long, formidable, final straightaway on the grassy, horse-trodden course required patience, perseverance, and a definite plan, and no one knew that better than a twenty-three-year-old farm boy from Illinois. His name is Craig Virgin, and this was his best race.

As a teenager growing up on the family farm in Lebanon, Illinois, Craig burst onto the national scene when he set the American high school record for the two-mile run. He would go on to win nine Big Ten championships and an NCAA cross-country title for the University of Illinois. When he arrived in Paris for the World Cross-Country Championship, he knew no American male had ever won that event, so he was looking for any advantage he could get. "I flew into Paris Thursday night so I had Friday and Saturday to go over the course before the race on Sunday," says Craig. "I knew that the last straightaway was very long, almost 800 meters, but I had something like that on my home course back at the University of Illinois. I ran the loops and then put on my spikes to practice that last straightaway several times. I knew that I had to have two or three gear changes: one from the final turn coming in after a slight incline, another somewhere between 200-300 meters from the finish, and maybe one more if I was close to the lead or had someone right behind me. So I mentally established landmarks for each of those gear changes."

Although many associate the Longchamp name with luxury handbags, horse racing aficionados know it as a famous racecourse along the banks of the Seine. Longchamp held its first race in 1857 and every year hosts the Prix de l'Arc de Triomphe, one of the most prestigious horse races in the world. But on Sunday, March 9, 1980, equine thoroughbreds gave way to the two-legged variety for 7.5 miles of championship cross-country running. Like in many horse races, there was trouble right out of the gate. "I was the captain and had to get my teammates situated at the starting line," says Craig. "When the gun went off I got out great, but then they fired the gun again for a false start. We were back at the line and I had my back to the field because I was trying to make sure everyone was set again. This time the starter didn't say 'ready' or 'set,' he just shot the gun and my own guys almost ran over me. I went down and someone grabbed me from behind and helped me as I staggered to my feet.

"There are moments of truth in every race," says Craig, "and that was one of them. I was really proud of this race because I faced several moments of truth in which I could have chickened out and played to my weaknesses and my fears, and instead I was able to hang tough and fight my way through those moments of doubt and fear. The first critical decision was in those first 800 meters after the trouble at the start when I was well back of the leaders. There were runners eight across in front of me so there weren't going to be many good chances to pass, and I thought about giving up and just throttling back and running just to finish. But then I thought that I didn't come 3,000 miles to do that so I decided to hang in there. We had seven miles to go and a lot can happen."

Longchamp Racecourse is actually four courses of various lengths. Runners not only had to negotiate the thick grass of the European-style track, but several hurdles along the prescribed route. Finding himself so far behind at the start, Craig spent the first half of the race moving up one place at a time like a jockey patiently picking his way through the field. "I just bided my time and looked for openings," says Craig, "and whenever there was one I'd accelerate and go through it. Finally with two laps to go I had worked my way through to the lead pack. I settled in at the back of that pack and looked ahead to see Nick Rose seventy meters out in front. I knew Nick from his long, blond hair and from being rivals in previous races."

Trying to recover from the effort he expended to reach the lead pack, Craig faced a second moment of truth in the race. "I had a difficult decision to make," he recalls. "Do I stay in the safety of the lead pack or do I take off after the leader? I knew Nick was tough and I could just stay where I was and aim for a top five finish, but instead I decided to slingshot around the pack and start off on my own. That was my first gear change. I would focus on watching Nick's cadence and make sure that my cadence was faster than his. My goal was to be on his shoulder with a lap to go and then make contact, hang on, then pick a moment in that last lap where I could try and break him or outsprint him. So I started closing the gap and little by little I could feel him coming back to me. As we came up the little hill I had closed the gap between us to about twenty yards, but just before the start of the final lap, Nick looked over his shoulder, saw me coming up on him, and took off in a sprint. Suddenly it was like all the adrenaline drained out of my body." And not only was Nick Rose lengthening the gap between them, three other runners were coming up behind Craig.

"I felt so vulnerable and I was sucking air trying to recover," he says. "I thought I was going to be hung out to dry." Then came a third moment of truth for Craig. "I thought about just giving up and going through the motions on that last lap as best I could and not fight any more. Others would say I came close but at least I gave it the old college try. But I decided that when those guys came up on me, I would try to hold on to them and not let them get by me, and that's what I did. I just ran with them and didn't let them pass me. I hung on to them like a drowning man on a life preserver." Fortunately, Craig had been doing fartlek training and hill repeats as part of his training, with the expectation he would need to recover on the run from the surges he and others would initiate during the race. "After about 300 yards I started to recover as the acid in my body equalized and was able to get back in a tempo."

Craig and the three other runners were now on the backstretch chasing Nick Rose, who had a fifty-yard lead, although the gap was not getting any wider. It was then that Craig noticed a sign of weakness in the leader. "We came to the far end of the course where there is a slight uphill climb before the final turn, and as Nick was going up that hill I thought I could detect a slight lag in his stride. I had run against him for five or six years and knew when he was running well and when he wasn't. His shoulders were coming up and he looked tense and I just felt he was looking tired and vulnerable." Perhaps also noticing vulnerability in the leader was Hans Orthmann of West Germany who surged past Craig and the others to close the gap. As Craig remembers, "Based on all the practice I'd done over that final straightaway, my gut was telling me it's just too far out yet. I decided it was too soon to make a move and I had to let Orthmann go."

"The West German is leading the charge now. This is really pulsating. He's closing the gap now. There are 500 meters to go and Nick Rose is

getting tired. It will be a tragedy for the man who has led so far."

"Up ahead I could see Orthmann gradually coming up on Nick's shoulder and battling for the lead and the crowd was just roaring. Finally with about 400 yards to go Orthmann took the lead and that's when I changed gears a second time. I told myself I had to change my form from a distance runner to a sprinter, so I put my head down and tried to lean forward and shorten my stride and pump my arms harder. I remember the grass was very thick with hoof prints in it and I had to search for that groove where it was firmer.

"I approached Nick and didn't hesitate but shot right past him and then came up behind Orthmann. By then it was a matter of where the finish line was and where he was and how much time I had. You pull the trigger and sometimes it works and sometimes it doesn't. That day it worked. I felt myself getting faster and I pulled in straight behind him where he couldn't see me. Then he looked left and I went right. I saw his head turn to the left and that's when I made my move to the right along the rail. And that's when I found one more little gear inside me and I just drove past him. If you're going to pass somebody you have to do it decisively so you can break them mentally and emotionally."

"Craig Virgin is overtaking Orthmann, a big grin on his face. He's timed it immaculately. He crept out of the pack earlier and edged his way through and he's the man showing the greatest form now. He's finishing with sprinting speed."

"I felt like I just exploded by and put five yards on him, but with about fifteen meters out I was feeling like I was about to run out of gas and I just kept pumping my arms looking for the finish. Then it was right upon me and I crossed the line and threw up my hands. I realized I had just pulled off a huge upset being the first American man to win. As I said, I was really proud of that race. It was huge for me."

Craig Virgin remains the only American male to ever win the World Cross-Country Championship. For good measure, he won it again the following year!

Running Tip: "Establish landmarks in the final half mile of a race where you want to change gears and build towards an all-out finish, just in case you are in a 'fatigue fog' at the end or are challenged in a tough race."

Paul Gompers

"Running is very much an individual sport where you take satisfaction in terms of improving yourself," says Paul Gompers. "But without sharing those successes with others it's a lot less meaningful. I was fortunate to be able to share my successes with my parents and my father in particular." Both parents regularly made the trek to Paul's competitions in high school and in college where he ran on Harvard's track team. Encouraged by his son's successes, Stephen Gompers started running himself, and eventually completed two marathons. In August 1985, before he was to leave for the World University Games in Japan, Paul ran a final tune-up race after which father and son went for an easy cooldown jog together. When they returned to the finish area, Stephen Gompers felt light-headed, collapsed, and died of a massive heart attack. He was forty-three.

"I was very close to my father," says Paul. "I shared a lot with him, including a love of sports, and without him following me to my races and supporting me, he would never have become interested in running. It was a very formative time to have something ripped away from me in a moment, to know my father wouldn't be there to support me anymore." Fortunately Paul did have the support of his teammates from the Harvard track and cross-country teams. "Runners know how close friendships are with people on a team," he says. "My teammates and my coach came out and supported me at the funeral. My coach took me on a twenty-mile run, and it was a run where we said nothing to each other, but it was just what I needed at the time. I can't imagine getting through it if I didn't have those kinds of friends."

Due mainly to his setting of the world junior record in the marathon (2:15:36) two years earlier, Paul had been selected to represent the United States in the World University Games in Kobe, Japan. But the timing could not have been worse. With the prospect of having to fly halfway around the world to run a marathon just weeks after his father's death, Paul was unsure what to do. "About five days after my father passed away I had a discussion with my mother about whether I should go to the Games," he recalls. "She said, 'You trained hard and your father was your biggest fan and he would want you to go,' so that's what I did. I was able to arrange to arrive a week after the rest of the team since the marathon was near the end of the Track & Field competition. It was hard to focus, but I decided I wanted to do something that honored the memory of my father and what he meant."

The World University Games are held every two years for university athletes in various sports. Both graduate and undergraduate students may compete, and Paul clearly felt at a disadvantage in terms of experience. "The only marathon I had done was in my sophomore year when I set the world junior record. The Italians had Orlando Pizzolato, who was in grad school and had won the New York City Marathon the year before. Another Italian, Salvatore Nicosia, was a twenty-eight minute 10,000-meter runner, and the Japanese had a couple of 2:10 marathoners on their team. So the field was actually quite strong. Not knowing really what to expect, my strategy was just to try and stay with the lead. As opposed to other races where you're focused on your competition, I would say that even more so I was focused on not letting my father down," says Paul. "That was the motivator in terms of getting me to the starting line, and was something that took on a life of its own within the race."

Once on that starting line, Paul and the other runners would have been forgiven for having second thoughts about running a marathon in Kobe, Japan in August. "It was incredibly hot," Paul recalls. "I think the race started a 6:00 a.m., and even then it was ninety degrees. At the end of the day the high temperature had peaked near one hundred, so as you might expect it was going to become a war of attrition. It wasn't going to be a fast race and no one was going to set a personal best.

"All along the way I was monitoring the people around me and how I felt, and I felt increasingly confident. If you looked on paper, there were at least fifteen guys with faster marathon personal bests than me in the race. Relatively speaking I was feeling good as they were dropping away and the pack kept dwindling. There were times where, had I not been focusing on my father, I may have slowed down. But I just kept pushing myself the entire time, being pushed by the thought that this was truly honoring my father. It was a way to start saying, 'Okay, I can go on with the rest of my life and my father won't be here, but this is a way to punctuate everything he meant to me up to that point in my life.' I wanted to do the best that I could. I ended up sticking near the lead and by about mile fourteen it was just me and Pizzolato. We were running at about a two-hour, twenty-minute marathon pace, which wasn't particularly fast, but the conditions were brutal."

Ten more miles of running in those conditions with the former (and future) winner of the New York City Marathon, however, began to take their toll. "I stayed side by side with Pizzolato until mile twenty-four, and then the wheels came off the wagon," says Paul. "There was just no way to stop it. I was light-headed and cramping and staggering from side to side, and then I was passed by the other Italian." Though he is convinced he took as much fluid during the race as his body could hold, Paul says he was dehydrated, a condition he had suffered only once before in a race. "I completely started bonking," he says. "I was very light-headed and started cramping. Like the flip of a switch you go from running 5:30 per mile pace to running 6:30 pace. From then on it was one foot in front of the other. You're counting street poles and the finish can't come soon enough. Focusing on those last two miles took a lot of concentration, but I told myself, 'This is for my father and I'm going to do this.' I was going to get to that finish line if I had to crawl. When I did get to the line, I immediately collapsed and was taken to the medical tent. I had given it one hundred percent of what I had. There was nothing left." Paul held on for third place with a time of 2:22.

"In the medical tent I got an IV and they put ice bags on me, and as my faculties came back to me I started to cry," he says. "In some ways, leaving so soon after the funeral and coming to Japan made it seem like it could have been a dream, then everything really hit me at that point. I felt I had put all my effort into the race, but it was also the realization that when I went back home my father wouldn't be there."

Paul finished his collegiate career at Harvard as a two-time All-American, and still holds the school record in the 10,000 meters. In the 1988 Olympic Trials he was slowed by an injury and finished fourth in the marathon, one spot away from making the Olympic team. These days Paul is back at his alma mater as a professor of business administration, and continues to be involved in the running program as a faculty fellow of the track team. "I still have this really strong connection to the team as a professor here. It's one of the things that defines who I am."

Looking back on that race from twenty-eight years ago, Paul was grateful for the opportunity to relive it as a way to reflect and keep the memory of his father alive. "At the end of the day, for me at least, my race at the University Games really began the healing process and was one way I could say goodbye to my father, who was a tremendous supporter and who was always there for me. While it was not my best athletic performance, it is certainly the most memorable and most meaningful race I have ever run because it was a way for me to honor him. It meant a lot to me to do that."

Running Tip: "Don't underestimate the importance of rest. It's the thing I didn't do enough of when I was competing. The one thing I learned, over time and through a variety of injuries, is that there are times when you really need to rest and to listen to your body."

Molly Huddle

African runners had just swept the top three places in the women's 5,000-meter run. After catching their breath, congratulating each other, and taking a final look at the scoreboard, they were about to walk off the track when they saw another runner celebrating. "Why is the American so happy," they were probably thinking. "Didn't she just finish *tenth*?"

The American *did* finish tenth that day at King Baudouin Stadium in Brussels. In fact, "I pretty much got my butt kicked," she says. But at the end, all that mattered to her was four hundredths of a second. On that day in that race, Molly Huddle broke the American record in the 5,000-meter run literally by the blink of an eye. The record, however, was not the only reason the race is so meaningful to her; it was what she learned along the way that made it possible. "My performance was the end result of a track season that had a steep learning curve, and I feel I used everything I learned that year in that race and it paid off for me."

So, just what was it the nine-time All-American, seven-time USA Road Race Champion, and future Olympian learned that she didn't already know? For one, she discovered she had a kick. Molly had done some serious training at altitude in the spring, covering about seventy-five miles a week with long runs in the fifteen-mile range, but "I really couldn't tell what kind of shape I was in," she says. "I wasn't hitting my times and it felt like every workout was difficult." Going into the US 5K Championships that summer, she still didn't feel in top form until later in that race. "Once we started kicking, I began to pick people off and I eventually finished second," she recalls. "I didn't really know

I had that kind of kick. I think it came from the training I did at altitude and the strength workouts my coach had us doing."

It was at a race in Paris a few weeks later that Molly first broke fifteen minutes in her specialty. "I surprised myself then and felt I could run even faster and be more aggressive, especially in the last two kilometers when the pace really starts dropping." In her next European race, Molly decided to go out and force the pace, knowing she finally had a legitimate chance at the 5K American record. "That didn't work," she says. "I realized that instead of forcing anything I had to just go with the flow and let the race happen in front of me. At the 3K mark runners are going to take off and things are going to start to hurt and I just had to be ready for that."

The European events in which Molly ran were Diamond League races known for their elite field of runners. "It's special any time I can get into a Diamond League race because it's high caliber competition and there's always a chance to run fast," she says. "I was lucky enough to get into three Diamond League races that year. I learned a little bit in every one and raced better in the last one than I did in the other two." But aside from the tactical racing experience gained on the track that year, Molly learned some valuable lessons from racing in Europe that had nothing to do with when to kick, when to be aggressive, or when to run with patience. They were "little things" as she says, but maybe those little things were worth four hundredths of a second off her finishing time. "From my experience in Europe I learned there's a whole new side of running. You really have to take care of things so you can go to a race feeling your best; little details that helped me feel good that day. You have to be fit, but you also have to show up without any issues like being out of alignment from traveling or being dehydrated, just little things like that."

Those little things may be foreign to most of us, but they can be critical to an elite runner's performance. "I had to go the extra mile when I arrived at the hotel to make an appointment with the chiropractor, take regular ice baths, and get massages. These were things I brushed off before because I didn't think they mattered, or I was just lazy. Now, if I just feel a little better, even if the benefit is just mental, it goes a long way. I really had to manage myself well because usually we don't have anyone to plan all that for us. But it is important. I think doing all that helped me get that last little one percent."

The final Diamond League race of the year was the Memorial Van Damme in Brussels, Belgium. "The stadium in Brussels was awesome, and there was a party atmosphere the whole time. The race was very deep with a lot of Kenyan and Ethiopian girls. In European races the runners are just going so fast you don't want to overthink it. I was very fortunate during the race because it was run on a pace that was close to what I wanted." What Molly wanted was a pace that would bring her in at least seven seconds under her personal best of 14:51, which she ran weeks earlier in another European meet. A time of 14:44 flat would break the American record of 14:44.80 held by Shalane Flanagan. "I had to let the race happen in front of me, but be ready when others began taking off in the last 2,000 meters, and then try my hardest to keep the gap between us small.

"I was lucky in that it was a smooth but fast pace. We were running pretty much 71- and 72-second laps the whole time, and the others really took off in the last mile. I was just keeping focused on staying as close to them as I could. I really felt pretty good because I had the confidence that I could stay with an elite field for at least 3,000 meters since I had done it before. But I knew for every lap, especially the last lap, I would have to push as hard as I could and not let up at the finish line; if I was going to break the record it was going to be really close. That record time was really stretching my capabilities.

"I'm usually on the pessimistic side when I'm racing, but at 3,000 meters I thought I was going to do it; that's being pretty confident for me." Confident or not, Molly admits that a habit of hers could have derailed any chance at a record. "I stayed out at the edge of lane two the whole way, which is not the best place to be for efficiency. I tend to do that a lot in order to stay out of trouble and away from runner's elbows, but I probably waste a little energy doing it."

Coaches were not allowed close enough to the track to shout advice to their runners or inform them of their times, but Molly seemed to have it all figured out. "I was keeping tabs and with 600 meters to go I calculated what I had to do to close," she recalls. "I needed to run my last lap in sixty-six seconds, but I realized a sixty-six-second lap feels a lot harder than usual when it's at the end of a 5K! I just tried to go as fast as I could at the end because I knew it might come down to the last decimal place. When I crossed the line I knew I had gotten the record, but it took some time for the result to come up on the scoreboard. They were ushering us off the track but I wanted to see what I had run." Then the time of 14:44.76 was posted next to Molly's name, making her the new American record holder by 0.04 seconds.

"It was weird because you envision yourself finishing among the top runners when you have run for a record," she says, "but the TV coverage didn't even show me finish because I was so far back. It was kind of an anticlimactic celebration. My parents and coach and husband watched it online back home so they knew about it, but I was pretty much the only one at the stadium who knew I broke the record." Molly still holds the record she set in Brussels, and says the confidence she gained from that race eventually helped her realize a lifelong dream when she qualified for and competed in the 2012 Olympics.

Looking back on that record-breaking performance in Brussels, she says, "I definitely have fond memories of that day. It was probably my worst placing ever in a race, but it was my best race."

Running Tip: "In a race you're trying to finish ahead of as many people as you can, so focus more on the competition than on your time. In the end, you may not only place higher but will often have a good finishing time too."

Steve Scott

"I kind of put a little bit of pressure on myself, almost like Babe Ruth when he pointed to the stands to indicate he was going to hit a home run." But Steve Scott was not talking about baseball; he was talking about running a mile. And not just any mile; a mile under four minutes. In his stellar career, the USA Track & Field Hall of Famer ran 136 sub 4-minute miles, more than any other person in history. None of those miles were more difficult, however, than the one he ran at the Drake Relays. When an illness kept him from running his event the first time, he promised the Drake fans he would return a year later to let them witness a sub 4-minute mile. Now, the year was up, the weather was atrocious, and Steve was nowhere near top form. Good luck with that.

No one who knew Steve Scott as a runner in high school would ever have imagined him being ranked as the number one miler in the US for eight straight years and holder of the US outdoor mile record (3:47.69) that stood for twenty-five years. By his own admission, he was an underachiever. "At that time in California there were a ton of good runners," he says, "but they all trained hard. I really didn't train that hard. All through high school I wouldn't run on weekends or during the summer like I was supposed to. The motivating factor for me to go out for track in the first place was to get a varsity letter to impress girls." The only college showing any real interest in Steve as a runner was the University of California at Irvine. As Steve recalls, "They had a fairly new program and were not very good, and that's where I ended up going."

Evidently, the UC Irvine coach saw something in Steve

that others did not. "He realized I was way underdeveloped," says Steve. "I was a very low-mileage guy with no consistent year-round training. Some of my contemporaries were running 80- to 100-mile weeks, and I was lucky if I was getting 30 or 40. But he saw definite potential in me based on how well I did in cross-country and the raw speed I had on the track with such limited training. I just needed to get a work ethic and to find the motivation to go out and train hard." Fortunately, Steve found that and more at the small Division II school, where he excelled first in the 800 meters and later in the mile and 1,500. "UC Irvine was definitely the right choice for me," he recalls. "I honestly believe I wouldn't have progressed had I been anywhere else but Irvine. I was in a low-key environment and was able to increase my dedication over time and with great people. My teammates were my mentors and taught me what real training was like. If I had first gone to a Division I school and compared myself to that level of competition, it would have been overwhelming."

Eventually, it was Steve Scott who began overwhelming the competition. While at UC Irvine he ran his first sub 4-minute mile, and by his senior year he had lowered his time in that distance to 3:53. Many meets across the country were eager to have a current and future star on their program, and the Drake Relays was one of them. Held on the campus of Drake University in Des Moines, Iowa, the Drake Relays is one of the most popular and prestigious track events in the country. When the meet director sent an invitation, Steve and his coach accepted. "The day that we left to fly to Des Moines for the Relays I had a fever of 104, says Steve. "I had a day to sleep but the next day I still had a bad fever. The meet director asked if I could at least come to the track to prove to the people that he wasn't making it all up. So I came out and they introduced me and I got on the sound system. I said that I was really sorry I couldn't run that year and then I guaranteed I would come back the next year and break four minutes for the mile. The crowd just went crazy."

Over the next year Steve graduated from UC Irvine and increased his total of sub 4-minute miles to 15. Did he remember his pledge to the fans? "I knew the whole year that I was going to have to run the Drake Relays that next spring, and that I had to break 4 minutes for the mile," he recalls. But springtime is typically not when world-class runners are at their best; most don't reach top form until the summer and Steve was no exception. When asked about his training leading up to the Drake Relays, Steve didn't have to guess; he just pulled out his old training log from more than thirty years ago. "In mid-April of that year I was not doing any track training yet. My peak time was going to be in the summer when I'd be going over to Europe. You're training for July and August, which is when the big European races are, so I was just in my base training. I was mainly doing long mileage (15-mile long runs) and hill repeats, but not much else." Turning the pages of the old training log, he realized his first quality speed session on the track (20 laps with a 200-yard jog in between) had been only two weeks prior to the meet. Going back to the baseball analogy, it was as if Steve had just begun swinging the bat after a long layoff, but was expected to hit a home run two weeks later in his first at-bat.

"So the next year comes along and I remembered my promise and went out to Des Moines for the purpose of running a sub 4-minute mile," he says. Knowing he would need all the help he could get, he brought former teammate Ralph Serna with him to be his pacesetter. "The day we arrived was beautiful," Steve recalls. "The next day was beautiful too, but the day the mile was going to be held was cold, windy and blustery, just a horrible day. It was definitely not sub 4 weather." And without the months of speed workouts that would normally bring him to mid-season form, "I just had to run on strength," he says.

"The gun went off and Ralph went into the lead but was having a tough time cutting through the wind because he's just a tiny guy," recalls Steve. He took me through the first lap in a little under 60 seconds, and the half mile in about two minutes. Ralph was supposed to set the pace for three laps but after that second lap he began to fall off. So now I was out there by myself. The one thing that is different about the Drake Relays compared to most other meets is that the people are knowledgeable about what's going on. It's not like an Olympic crowd where they don't really know anything about track. In Des Moines they know what the good marks are and they know who the top people are and they appreciate it. So in that third lap people just started going nuts. As I ran around the track they started clapping in unison. It became a thunderous roar and their applause really lifted me.

"I went through the third lap right around 3 minutes or 3:01, and I knew the crowd could sense that it was difficult for me," he says. Difficult not just because of the cold and windy conditions, but because Steve had no serious rivals that day; no one was nipping at his heels providing an incentive to run fast in order to win. "Usually it's because there is competition that I have to run fast times to win the race," he says, "but in this situation there wasn't anybody with me. I was probably fifty yards ahead of the next runner and it's a lot tougher that way." When Steve would find himself in that same situation at other races, he says he would probably not put forth the effort but shift to a lower gear for the certain victory. But he admits when the crowd got behind him in Des Moines, he felt obliged to run fast, and even faster than he had planned.

"On the last lap the crowd was going absolutely bananas. I couldn't hear myself think, and I really thrived off of it. If I walk into a stadium and there's no noise, it's like I don't care. But if the fans are into it, I get pumped up. They realized that I was hurting and they just took me all around the track. Even though it was pretty windy I felt like I was floating those last 400 yards, and I ended up running 3:56 in horrible conditions. It really was the crowd. The third and fourth laps were the ones when the crowd kept me going. With the weather and the kind of shape I was in, I shouldn't have been able to run that fast. They inspired me. The rest of my time in Des Moines, it was like I was king for a day. Wherever I went, people recognized me and congratulated me. It was an awesome experience."

Fifteen years after that race, at the age of thirty-eight, Steve was diagnosed with cancer. Though the operation was a success, he was never able to attempt his goal of running a sub 4-minute mile at the age of forty. With his fast times behind him, the current track coach at Cal State San Marcos now runs mainly to stay in shape. "It's just weight management now," he says. "If my weight starts going up, then I run more mileage, and if the weight comes down, I don't run much." Nevertheless, recreational runners everywhere can take heart in the fact that when the owner of 136 sub 4-minute miles does hit the roads these days, it's at the pleasant but pedestrian pace of seven and a half minutes per mile.

Running Tip: "The mistake that I made and others make is to always think more is better. You're better off doing one too few as opposed to one too many—in terms of miles, intervals, and races. Masters runners especially don't have to train harder as they get older, they just have to train more intelligently. As you get older, all that mileage is behind you. You can do one less hard workout a week and concentrate more on working yourself aerobically."

Ed Ayers

Ed Ayers had a secret: he was going to win the JFK 50-Mile run. Never mind that the JFK 50 is one of the most competitive and challenging races in the US, or that Ed had never won a big race before, or that he had run only one ultra-length race in his career. He was going to finish first, end of story. "It was almost a mystical feeling," says the founding editor of *Running Times* magazine. "I never had it before and never had it since. For the six or eight months leading up to the race, I just knew I was going to win it."

Of course, for someone to even make that assertion, they had to have some good credentials, like a personal best of 2:31 in the marathon. Indeed, Ed's time was just eight minutes above the cutoff that would qualify him to run in the 1976 Olympic Marathon Trials. "I was training seriously and my dream was to run a marathon fast enough to qualify me for those trials," he says. "But there's a saying that if you want to make God laugh, tell Him your plans." Ed's plan to lower his marathon time before the deadline was to select a race on a relatively flat out-and-back course. And just as planned, he was on pace to make that qualifying time when he arrived at the halfway point, thanks in part to a strong tailwind. Unfortunately, at the turnaround, that tailwind became a headwind, and his time slowed dramatically. A final chance at qualifying came at the Boston Marathon, but then heat, not wind, played the role of spoiler. "The temperature in Boston that day was over 100 degrees before the old traditional noon start," he recalls. "I was forced to run two minutes-per-mile slower than usual. My dream had been killed."

With the running boom of the mid-seventies came better

training techniques and tougher competition, and eventually Ed saw the writing on the wall. "Marathons were getting faster and faster by then and I discovered I just didn't have the leg speed or the right biomechanics to get much better." But he began hearing of events called ultramarathons, and something about those races that are *longer* than the 26.2-mile marathon distance resonated with him. "Hey, maybe that's for me," he recalls thinking at the time. On a whim he entered the national 50-Mile Championship in 1976, which was ten laps around New York's Central Park. He finished third. Even sweeter was when he caught and passed a runner who had been one of the select few to qualify for that year's Olympic Marathon Trial—the race Ed dreamed of running. "Passing him gave me a big psychological boost, and that race gave me the confidence that I could really run that 50-mile distance."

But Ed knew that running ten laps around Central Park is tame compared to competing in the JFK 50. The event began in 1963 as part of President Kennedy's push to promote physical fitness, and is the only race of its kind to be held every year since. Starting in the town of Boonsboro, Maryland, the 50-plus-mile course gains 1,172 feet in elevation in the first 5.5 miles, and traces the rocky, single-track Appalachian Trail for nearly thirteen miles. After dropping 1,000 feet through a series of steep switchbacks, runners connect with the historic C & O Canal Towpath, a long, unpaved, wind-in-your-face, 26.3-mile test of fortitude. "You just spent about two and a half hours on the rugged Appalachian Trail after a steep climb," Ed cautions, "and then on the towpath you have to run the equivalent of a marathon." As if that's not enough, there are still 8.4 miles of rolling country roads remaining until the finish.

Before ever hearing about the JFK 50, the lifelong environmentalist had often hiked and run along the Appalachian Trail and had an appreciation for the beauty and history in that part of the country. It was when a friend entered the 1977 race that Ed decided to join him, thinking, "It was going to be a good adventure." Sure, Ed had finished third in the National 50-mile Championship and, at age thirty-six, was in the peak year for an ultra runner in terms of physical capability. But there were about 450 other runners entered in that year's race, including many who had covered the demanding course multiple times. What was it that made Ed so sure he was going to finish first?

For one, everything was finally in balance. "In running, you need to get the right balance," he says, "and I was achieving a whole series of balances. I had found the right balance between endurance work and speed work, between youth and experience, and between confidence and a hunger to win a big race. It all came together, so I had some feeling I was going to run well. But it wasn't like back in high school when I knew I was going to do well by knowing the best times of my competitors. It wasn't prediction this time but knowledge; somehow I knew it would be my day. I had this secret that I was carrying, and that magical feeling stayed with me the whole distance." If there was any early indication it was indeed going to be Ed's day, one need only look at an old photograph taken of the leaders atop South Mountain just after the start. After a tortuous two-mile climb, Ed is the only one with a big grin on his face.

Ed hung with that lead group along the Appalachian Trail, taking a tumble once at fifteen miles but getting right back up. He was in fifth place when he arrived at the long and lonely C & O Canal Towpath. "Here the monotony can get to a lot of people," Ed admits, "but I never get bored with such a course. I can enjoy the surroundings and be stimulated by the beautiful scenery. Besides, the feeling of exhilaration that I was going through this wonderful adventure to win the race was able to override any feeling of monotony." Then at the 22-mile mark, Ed made a gutsy decision. "Approaching the aid station I was in second place, and I could see up ahead that the leader had stopped to refuel. I decided not to stop but kept going. That's always a gamble, especially in an ultra race, because you need to keep refueling and rehydrating, but I seized the opportunity to take the lead. From then on I was all alone."

In *The Loneliness of the Long Distance Runner*, Alan Sillitoe described what goes through a runner's mind when leading a race. But the working-class hero in that short story ran alone for only a few miles until the finish line; Ed still had twenty-eight lonely miles to cover. "I was thinking mainly of how damn good it felt," he recalls. "I just love the feeling of running when you're running well. I was in a wonderful place and was feeling good." That "good" feeling lasted until he came off the towpath with eight miles still to go. "I was starting to feel depleted, energy-wise, because I really hadn't refueled very much," he says, remembering the aid station he skipped in order to take the lead. "That was the one thing interfering with me. Then I began to feel a little concerned that someone might be coming up behind me." Help came in the form of a cookie. "My wife was waiting along the road at the 42-mile mark and I asked if she had anything I could eat. She gave me a cookie and it was great. Knowing what we do now about nutrition it may not have been the best way to refuel, but it was perfect at the time." Up ahead was a bend where Ed could catch a glimpse half a mile behind him through an open field. "I looked back and there was no one there.

"The finish was like a dream come true. I had known this for months and now it was really happening." Ed finished with a time of six hours and four minutes, about twelve minutes ahead of the second place finisher. "It's a rare feeling when everything is in synch, and that's how it was for me in that race," he says. "I never ran that fast again, but over the years my love of running has never faded. Now, over three decades later, when I enter a race as an 'old' man, I can draw inspiration from my own memory of that magical day."

Running Tip: "Be patient both in training and in racing. Don't rush your training in order to accumulate a good base of mileage, and don't go out too fast in a race or you will pay for it later."

Jenny Barringer Simpson

Jenny Barringer Simpson did the math and liked her odds. "I have a twenty-five percent chance of medaling tonight," she recalls thinking before the World Championship 1,500-meter final. "If there are only twelve of us, then one in four is going to walk away with a medal, so why not me?" A medal? Maybe. But the odds of that medal being gold were pretty slim. Jenny was clearly not one of the favorites in that strong international field, and history was definitely not on her side; she wasn't even born the last time an American woman won gold in that event on the world stage.

In college, the Economics and Political Science major was used to winning, but her race was the steeplechase, not the 1,500. "I really found an identity with the steeplechase," she says, "and I committed to it for four years. The special skill the steeplechase gave me was that it taught me how to win and how to go into every race expecting to perform at a certain level." But even three-time NCAA and two-time USA champions need a change at some point in their careers, so Jenny eventually looked for another event to which she could make a similar commitment. "After college it was time to challenge myself and move onto something different," she recalls, "so I moved to Colorado Springs and worked with 1,500-meter specialist Juli Benson. It was a great fit right from the beginning."

A new coach and a new race meant a new training regimen, although Jenny stayed true to her old principles when it came to workouts. "Every day when I'm out training, I'm out working hard to win races," she says. "Running is really fun, winning is way better. The combination of the two can't be matched. That

79

being said, I don't think I've ever gone to practice saying I'm doing this so I can win a world championship." For Jenny, a regimen of short sprints, long runs, threshold runs, fartlek, 800- and 1,000-meter repeats, dynamic drills, and weight lifting was all part of a typical training week. "The combination of training and confidence from years of running in college gave me a good demeanor and a good aggressive attitude leading up to the World Championships," she says. It was an attitude she needed just to survive qualifying for those championships, where she made the team by finishing second. "Qualifying is so intimidating. It's the worst part of the whole process. Exciting, but cutthroat."

Two more cutthroat rounds awaited the athletes after they arrived in Daegu, South Korea for the World Championships. As Jenny recalls, "My goal was to make the final. I knew if I could do that I could leave saying at least I had a shot at doing well. The main observation from some of the others that week was that I got better as I went through each round. I was still inexperienced in the 1,500 but my coach reinforced a trait in me that you can always learn from yourself no matter if you have an hour or two days or two years to get it right. I barely made it through the first round, but made it very comfortably in the second round. I was making better decisions and building confidence through the course of those five days."

Critical in helping Jenny make better tactical decisions was the knowledge gained from watching the race videos with her coach after each round. "We would see what decisions different runners made, what decisions I made, and how I could do it better next time," she says. "Seeing my race from a spectator's point of view rather than from the thick of the pack really showed me how my decision making affected my race. I learned a lot about who looks tentative, who looks strong, who wants to run on the inside or outside." But perhaps the greatest lesson she learned leading up to the final was to remain calm, especially in the frantic final lap. "Watching the race video reinforced that when you feel really boxed in at the bell, don't panic," she says. "Some runners panic, but the group does shift around and it does open up. You have sixty seconds to work out your situation, and you see in the video how it opens up and there is always going to be a way out if you're smart about it."

Jenny laughs when asked if the other runners in the final were wary of her. "I definitely was not one of the favorites," she says. "I was with a different coach, at a different training venue, and running a different race, so I wasn't on many people's radar. I can look back to the starting line on a lot of important races and I remember here thinking that this was my first World Championship 1,500 and nobody would have thought I was even going to make it to the final. I know it sounds corny, but I remember feeling really proud of myself." Jenny also remembers the slow pace once the race got underway. "We got to the 100-meter mark and everyone hit the brakes," she recalls. "I was toward the back so I swung out and came near the front of the pack. Being in second place after 125 meters meant nothing, but for me it set the tone. It was different for me from other races where I would just sit around and see what people did and be intimidated. I wanted to get some mental contact with the front of the pack and set the tone that for me this was the top group. I didn't stay up with them but my mind was connected with that group the entire run.

"I don't remember much about the next two laps and what decisions I made, but I do remember getting to the bell lap—I think I was in 8th place—and thinking to just stay on the rail for another curve and be as efficient as possible ... and don't panic. I stayed on the rail for one more turn and waited until the backstretch to get into a better position. I think that small decision to wait was really influenced by watching those videos and learning not to panic, and learning that things would eventually open up. Even though it was a small thing, I think it really made the race for me."

Jenny did not panic, but instead waited for the opening she knew would come. "Then this perfect spot opened up and it was just beautiful," she recalls. "I was able to fade to the outside and get as much track as I needed to go around people. With 200 meters to go I decided to just run as hard as I could. We got up to the top of the curve and I was still on the outside. I wasn't thinking about beating people at that point. I wasn't thinking about place. I was just thinking about running as hard as I could. I was totally focused about getting the most out of my body at that point, just trying to propel myself forward as quickly and aggressively as possible. There's a great picture of me with the rest of the group coming around the curve, and I think you can tell that our minds are at completely different places; every other face in that picture is straining, and I look like I'm daydreaming."

Spain's Natalia Rodgriguez was out front as the runners entered the final straightaway while Jenny gained ground on the outside. "We came around the curb and I was thinking that this is what it's like closing with world-class 1,500-meter runners. This is when everybody is going to run away from me. I was closing as fast as I could and was thinking more about my arms and my legs and pushing myself than worrying about catching one person or two people. I was expecting Rodriguez and all the others to take off but I remember everyone beginning to fade in my peripheral vision and thinking to myself, 'What is happening?' Then in the last twenty meters I knew I was winning and I just didn't know how to react. I couldn't believe it. When I crossed the finish line I remember my mouth was wide open and my eyes were so wide and I was totally speechless. I didn't know what you do when you win a World Championship. I remember one of the women from the race came over and gave me a hug, and I think she snapped me back to reality, and then I started jumping up and down."

With her victory, Jenny became the first US Women's World Champion in a middle distance since Mary Slaney won the 1,500 in 1983. But to Jenny, there are some things more precious than a gold medal. "Before the race I was thinking about my little sister," she says. "We were like typical siblings and didn't get along at all through our high school years. She had kind of a wayward life for a while but had enlisted in the army and was doing really well. It entered my mind that if I win, the national anthem will be played and I will be able to stand on the podium and share the national anthem with my sister in the military. I thought it would be such a cool gift to give her to share that moment with her. Four minutes earlier I was thinking about this at the starting line, and running down the straightaway I was thinking of her again. It ended up to be a really special thing that my sister and I were able to share together, and in the post-race interview I mentioned how proud I was of her and told everyone to sing the anthem loud for my sister. Days later when we talked, she said it really meant the world to her, and it has made us a lot closer."

Running Tip: "Focus on your own race and not on your competitors. You only have so much mental and emotional energy you can expend in your race. Try and maximize what you can get out of yourself. At least for me, if I'm not distracted by anything else, I can be proud of how I perform."

Miguel Galeana

"We had all come in different ways: my father did the desert thing, my mother did the tunnel thing, and we went over the fence into a waiting van." Miguel Galeana, now a US citizen and college graduate, was talking about his family's crossing over the border from Mexico. His mother's journey was especially treacherous, and her story would eventually become part of his best race.

Miguel and his siblings followed their parents to the state of Washington where Miguel's father already had a job in the lumber industry. "Since we were the first Hispanics in our community, our parents wanted us to get involved in athletics in order blend in," says Miguel. "I did every sport and running happened to be the one thing I could do extremely well." Eventually Miguel couldn't "blend in" any longer; he became too good a runner. State championships and a scholarship to Montana State followed, and after graduation the Asics-sponsored runner became known as one of the best in the region.

On the suggestion of a friend, Miguel entered the Chuckanut 7-mile trail race in Bellingham, Washington, a race that typically draws several elite-level runners. Starting in Marine Park, the point-to-point course follows the Interurban Trail through the Chuckanut Mountains before finishing in Larabee State Park.

"My experience in longer races was not great," says Miguel. "I was a miler and steeplechaser in college and seven miles was getting into that foreign territory for me." Another issue that concerned him was side stitches, something from which he suffered if he started too fast or if he surged too hard later in the race. "I couldn't start faster than five-minutes-per-mile pace or else I would get them," he says. "So anytime I was in a field that was going to start sub five, I knew I couldn't go out with them. I knew they could eventually come back to me, but it's never fun to watch someone take off and put twenty seconds on you right away."

As expected, two runners started fast and Miguel had to let them go. "Right after the start, the course makes a right turn then goes up a hill. Attacking the hill becomes a problem for someone prone to side stitches, so I had to back off even more. I stayed back with a chase group and within a quarter mile I was already behind by about 100 meters."

Until mile three the course is straight and narrow. Miguel was tucked in behind the chase group running at what he estimated was a five-minute pace. The leaders, still out of sight, were probably dashing through the woodsy course at close to 4:40 pace. "I wanted to get in front of the chase group before the big hill," says Miguel, "so I gradually picked up my pace. I would get the side stitches if I surged because I couldn't breathe fast enough. What I learned from running was about getting into a rhythm and not changing gears too much. I would just sustain a certain momentum."

The major feature of the Chuckanut course is what's known as California Hill, a steep, intimidating climb at the three-mile mark. According to Miguel, "You look at it and you think, 'That's not going to be fun.' You pretty much almost have to walk it. I jogged and walked, but I probably could have hiked it faster than running it. As I came to the base of the hill I could see the leaders just as they were getting over the crest of the hill, about to start a slight descent for four miles. I almost settled into the notion that I wasn't going to catch those guys."

Alone in third place, Miguel was already breathing hard as he began to walk and jog up California Hill. "I was just gritting my way up," he says. "It's one of those hills where you think you're done, but there's still a little bit left at the top to keep you from opening up your stride too soon. Once I got to the top of the steepest part, there were still about fifty more meters of gradual climb. Then you get to what you were waiting for the whole time, which is a beautiful descent with four miles to go. I reached the top and took a couple of deep breaths, and that's when I realized that going up that hill had made my shoulders and my back really tight."

Despite the tightness on his body, Miguel opened up the pace and resorted to a personal racing strategy that had served him well in races since college. He called it "running scared." "If I don't want the group behind to catch me, or I know there is a group in front of me, my mind starts to think, 'How can I make myself go faster? How do I keep the momentum going?' I always tell the athletes I coach to pretend somebody's coming up on them, and run scared. At this point I was running scared as a way of pushing the pace."

The next two miles on the course were quiet, dark, and lonely along a section of railroad track. Miguel kept looking ahead for the leaders, for any indication he had made up some ground on them, but they remained out of sight. "I was pushing the pace and when the course turned I still couldn't see anyone up ahead, then I got a side stitch," he recalls, "and I knew what was coming afterwards. Every time I got a side stitch I also feel a nerve pinching on my right shoulder. I was poking at the stitch and taking deep breaths and holding it in, but things just got worse. The pain traveled from my shoulder to my hand and then my whole arm felt paralyzed. I was still running and gritting my teeth, but that was my first experience with pain at that level. Nothing was working. My arm was just done."

Aching from the side stitch, the numbness in his arm, and the pain and tightness in his shoulders and back, Miguel's mind wandered. "For whatever reason I went to my mother's trip," he remembers clearly. "I started to think of the story my parents had told me of how my mother came to the States in 1980. The pain took me there. My father lived and worked in Washington for a year to raise the money to get my mother to the States (and later the children). As I ran with my pain I started to picture my mother coming across the border. My mother was the only woman in the group of twelve people and had to endure a journey with the ones paid to bring her across ("Coyotes") in terrible heat. The most terrifying part of the journey was a mile-long tunnel, which they traveled through in the middle of the night. The tunnel began about five feet high, but the farther they went into it the darker and smaller it got. At times my mother had to get on her hands and knees to crawl, and sewage water came up to her neck. She crawled with all those men worried about being raped or worse, and the only thing that kept her from losing her mind were thoughts about her children and the better life she hoped to give them.

"As I raced I pictured her journey and imagined all the pain and emotions she had gone through. I asked myself if my side stitch and shoulder pain could compare to her misery when she was crawling through that tunnel and missing her children (he stops to compose himself). I told myself that I was being a pansy, and as soon as I saw a sign indicating a dip in the trail (1.5 miles to go) I came out of my thoughts. All I know is that when I stopped thinking about my mother's story and saw the trail open up to the light, the pain was gone, and I couldn't remember running that previous mile."

Just then the leaders emerged around the next turn, much closer than they had been earlier in the race. "It was like someone had given me oxygen," says Miguel. "I felt a surge of energy and lighter on my feet. I sprinted down the next little hill and attacked the following hill, and at that point I knew if I was going to do anything, that was the time to do it. The rule for me is if the hill is close to the end you attack it; if it comes early in the race, you don't. Just over the crest of the hill I caught the two leaders. I looked at them and noticed they were hurting. I didn't say anything to them, but in my mind I was thinking, 'You guys made me hurt, so now I'm going to punish you.' After a few seconds running alongside them I just opened up and ran the fastest mile I've ever done at the end of a race. As soon as I heard the band I knew I was getting close to the finish, and then the course opened up to this beautiful park. My first thought was, 'Did I just run that last mile that fast, and how did I recover from that pain so quickly?' My time was a course record.

"Ever since that race I go back to those thoughts of my

mother's journey whenever I have a hard time at anything, not just in a race. Since then we finally sat down and talked about her trip and my trip to the States in a way we hadn't before. She has been the most amazing person to me because of what she had to endure, and her life has been devoted to taking care of us. I won that race because of her."

Running Tip: "Plan a strategy and don't forget to execute that plan in the race. You can't go into a race and just wing it."

George Hirsch

"My best race? That's easy. It's the one where I met my wife."

George Hirsch, Chairman of the New York Road Runners and former publisher of *Runner's World*, never intended to run the New Jersey Waterfront Marathon that day. He wasn't registered, wasn't trained, and obviously wasn't watching his caloric intake after polishing off a big buffet breakfast. But George soon found himself on a mission, and nothing was going to stop him: a mission to find the woman who would eventually become the love of his life. Her name was Shay Scrivner, and through separate interviews, this is their story.

George: "The Meadowlands Complex in New Jersey was headquarters for the runner's expo the day before the marathon. I was at the *Runner's World* booth and this beautiful woman

89

walked by and we looked at each other. I had been married but had been single for quite a long time, and I think most of my friends thought that was the way I was going to stay. She kept walking and I followed her and then approached her and said, 'Hi.' She asked me if I was George Hirsch, and I would have said 'yes' no matter what!"

Shay: "I decided I was going to train for this marathon. I had run a few 5K races before and a half marathon, but I knew nothing about how you train to run 26.2 miles. A friend said, 'I know someone who can help you; his name is George Hirsch and he'll send you a training packet.' So eventually I received a thick manila envelope from *Runner's World* with information on how to train for your first marathon. I followed it religiously and then went to the expo the day before the race to pick up my number. I walked through the door and there in front of me was the *Runner's World* booth. I didn't read *Runner's World* and I didn't have a clue who he was. There were probably five people at the booth and four were under thirty, so I knew the last one had to be George. I was going to go up to him and thank him for sending me the information packet when we caught each other's eye. There was this electricity between us and the feeling was so strong it made me uncomfortable. So I walked around to go up the next aisle and then thought I was being stupid, and decided to go back and thank him. When I turned around he was following about two feet behind me. I asked him if he was George Hirsch, and he said, 'Yes.'"

George: "So I did the only thing I could do, which was to invite her to have dinner with me that night, but she said, 'No.' Wanting to keep the conversation going, I asked her about her plans for the race, and she said she just wanted to finish. She added that her goal would be to run the New York City Marathon in the fall and qualify for Boston. I asked her what time she needed and she said since she was forty years old she needed to run 3:40, so I remembered that. The next day I met Frank Shorter and some others for a meeting and we had a big buffet breakfast—waffles and pancakes and bacon and all that— before driving out to the starting line. I was doing commentary for NBC for the Olympics that summer and the race would be used as the Olympic Trials marathon, so I was just there to cover the race; I hadn't run a marathon in about four years. The trials race started fifteen minutes before the regular marathon, so we watched them start and then I walked into the sea of people who were getting ready to start the regular race and looked for Shay. The gun went off and I waited for every last person to cross the starting line, and when that happened I started jogging going left and then right and didn't see her. I kept running and running and finally just as I was getting to five miles, there she was up ahead. She had a headset on and I came up alongside her and tried to be extremely casual. I said, 'Hi, how are you doing?'"

Shay: "He came to the marathon to cover it as a journalist. He always wears his running shorts underneath and then usually his long running pants over that whenever he goes to a running event, like he did that day. And he always wears running shoes. It was my first marathon so I was totally focused on this race. Believe me, I hadn't given him another thought. I was at about five miles and all of a sudden he came up to me. I was totally surprised. He acted very cool and said, 'Hi.' I said, 'What are you doing here?' Then we just started talking about life and the times when we were children, and all the time I'm thinking about how he's going to get back. I didn't know if he was fit to run the whole way."

George: "I told her I was looking for her so I could say 'hello' to her again. We started talking and she asked how I was supposed to get back to the start. I told her not to worry, that I could hitch back. So we kept talking and one thing led to another and all of a sudden life stories were coming out of us. We never talked about her time, but I was thinking about it. I was remembering the 3:40 she needed to qualify for Boston. With about two miles to go the conversation died down and we were just focused on finishing. At 3 hours, 37 minutes, and 1 second she crossed the finish line and I stepped aside since I didn't have a race number. I was able to run the 3:37 comfortably. So at that point I knew a good amount about her. Then I went in one direction to get back to the press tent and she went in another."

Shay: "He actually stayed with me the entire race; he was so helpful. It was cold and it rained and it was windy; not a good day for your first marathon. We just talked and talked and I wasn't aware I was going that fast. He kept getting a little ahead of me so he was kind of pulling me along. He was probably keeping the same pace and I was not. At about mile 18 I told him I was getting tired and he said, 'It's a marathon, that's what happens in a marathon, you get tired.' But I got beyond that. Finally at twenty miles I was really running beyond what my capability was and I told him that if he was there to help me he better come back for me, so he put on the brakes and came back to me and that was very nice of him; that made an impression. And I guarantee you I would never have qualified for Boston had he not been setting the pace. It was beyond what I had trained for, but he pushed me over in a very nice way."

George: "At that point, ever since I had met her, I could think of nothing else. Early the next morning I was at my desk and the phone rang and it was her. She said she just wanted to thank me because she didn't have a chance to do it at the end of the race. Then she asked if there was a chance she could take me out to lunch because I helped her qualify for Boston. When we met for lunch the following weekend she said she was moving back to Idaho so the timing was wrong. As it turned out, she was going through a divorce so there was no interest on her part. So off she went and I couldn't get her out of my mind. But I had this feeling that somehow, some way, I was going to see her again."

Shay: "A week later I took him to lunch to thank him and he said he wanted to see me, but I was going through a divorce and did not need another relationship at that point. I was very insistent and he honored that. A week later I left New Jersey to return to Idaho. I wasn't thinking about him until the Olympics when he came on TV doing the commentating, and my two boys said, 'Mom, isn't that the guy who ran the marathon with you?' In December I came back to New York to talk to some publishers about a book I had written. I called him and said I would love to go for a run. He said he knew some good places to run, and that was the beginning."

George and Shay were married in 1989, and for twenty-five years after they first set eyes on each other they remained inseparable. George even slept on a cot beside his wife for fifty-six days while she recovered in the hospital from a bone marrow transplant. "He has been a wonderful partner in my life," says Shay. We're just two of the really fortunate and lucky people."

George made the 2009 New York City Marathon his final 26.2-mile race after promising his wife he wouldn't run any more marathons. He ran for a charity that benefits research into multiple myeloma, a blood cancer that Shay battled until her death in February, 2014.

Running Tip: "It's not likely that you will find the love of your life or win an Olympic gold medal, but try to go into every race well prepared with a plan for that day and an optimistic attitude. Then just let it unfold."

Ed Eyestone

As a youth, Ed Eyestone already had his future neatly planned out. "I was going to be a professional baseball player," he says. "I would make the Little League team, play in junior high and high school, and then get drafted right out of high school. I would get called up to the major leagues after a month in the minors, and it would be just a matter of time before I was Most Valuable Player of the World Series. All that went fine … until I was cut from the junior high school team." Baseball's loss was track and field's gain as Ed went on to become a ten-time All-American, a four-time NCAA champion, and a two-time Olympian. But before all that could happen, Ed Eyestone would have to meet Wayne Pinto.

After being cut from his baseball team, Ed considered his options. "I noticed for the first time in my life that there was another sport in the spring besides baseball," he says, "and that was track and field. I approached the coach and asked what I had to do to become a member of the team, and he said that if I came out and did the workouts he prescribed, I would make the team and there would be no cuts, so I thought that sounded good." Although he didn't become the best runner on his team until later, Ed started out as one of the hardest workers. "I knew I wasn't necessarily the fastest in terms of raw foot speed, but I knew I could try as hard as the next guy if not harder. I could beat most of the other seventh graders in the half mile and the mile, and as an eighth grader I could beat all the other eighth graders and most of the ninth graders. As a ninth grader I was the fastest guy in school."

It was at Bonneville High School in Washington Terrace,

Utah that Ed met the coach who saw his potential and became his mentor. "In high school my coach introduced me to the running culture and how cool it was to be a runner," he says. "I was hooked at that point. He would tell us stories, he would run with us, and he really wanted us to do as well as we could. As a result of his mentorship I felt like part of a family, and we all felt an allegiance to him. We would run through a wall for the guy. He would make us run over the summer and kept records of our summer workouts. When I entered my junior year he told me that, based on my workouts and the time trials I did, I was going to have a breakout year. A fifteen-year-old gets excited at that kind of news, especially when I had great expectations for myself and had never fulfilled any of them."

In the state of Utah in 1977, the dominant high school runner was a senior, a Navajo named Wayne Pinto who had not lost a race at any distance since he was a freshman. "He could win a race any way he wanted to," says Ed. "He could win a slow race because he had a killer kick, or he could win with a grinding hard pace from the gun and run away from everybody. Everyone in the state knew who he was because of his record. He was pretty much unbeatable and had the full bag of tricks. He spent summers on the Navajo reservation and there was a rumor he once ran down a deer, so there was this Native American mystique surrounding him too." When cross-country season got underway, the Bonneville team was doing a mix of hard/ easy days of training, consisting of hill work, long intervals, and longer runs. "By the time of the Kiwanis Cross-Country Invitational, the first big event of the season, my coach was confident in my abilities," recalls Ed, "or at least he made me feel he was confident in my abilities. As I was setting goals for myself for that race, I decided I just wanted to run *with* Wayne Pinto for as long as I could. Days later, on the school bus to the meet, a friend asked what my plan was and I told him I was going to run with Wayne Pinto ... and that I was going to try to *beat* him. I really felt like it was something I was capable of doing based on the good training I had. After we arrived at the site I looked out over the park and saw the ugly brown and yellow uniforms of

Wayne's Davis High School team. I was telling myself, 'Today I'm going to run with Wayne Pinto!' He wouldn't have known me from Adam because I was only fortieth in the state meet the year before and I had not really proven anything. The only ones who knew how good I was were my coach and I."

The two teams were at opposite ends of the wide field, separated by numerous other schools. When the gun sounded, Ed made sure to get out fast to the middle as the lead pack formed. "We all met in the middle and went out way too hard," says Ed. "I was happy to be in the lead pack and as I looked around, sure enough there was Wayne, probably two or three rows of people ahead of me. He had a compact trunk and piston-like legs. He wasn't leading the race but he was leading in the sense that everybody knew he was there and seemed just to be waiting for him to do something. At the mile mark he was running even with the guy in the lead and I wondered what kind of race it was going to be. Was he going to grind it out and kill us all early or was he going to play with us a little bit. It seemed that he wanted a fast, honest pace, so the lead pack got strung out to five or six guys behind Wayne, and I was one of them. I remember thinking, 'Okay, I'm running in the lead pack, this is cool.' We were running at a hard enough pace that my inner barometer was asking, 'Can I maintain this pace for three miles?' I hoped so, but I wasn't positive. I was in new, uncharted territory at that time because I had never run up front in a race like that before, and I hoped I could just hold on.

"At his particular course there was an area around the two-mile mark where spectators can congregate. As we came to that point, the pack was down to three of us, and I heard my dad yell the usual, 'Run him into the ground, Ed.' I never knew what that meant but it sounded cool. So now with a mile to go, things were intensified that much more because Wayne realized he still had a couple of people with him. Then at about the two-and-a-half-mile mark that third guy fell back and it was just me and Wayne Pinto. The race probably could have ended right there and it would have been a high-water mark in my career just to have hung with him that long, so that was very exciting.

"As fate would have it, we traversed this woodsy area with trees and roots and it seemed like Wayne caught a spike on one of those roots, causing just enough of a hitch in his stride that I drew dead even with him. With less than a half mile to go we were shoulder to shoulder. We made this big sweeping turn and I was on the inside so he had to run a little bit farther, and there was a long, gradual downhill to the finish. As we remained shoulder to shoulder, the good news for me was that I was a very good downhill runner for whatever freakish reason. Maybe because I was tall or because I had a tendency to go all out down hills without fear of falling. As we started down the hill I could tell with each stride that I was picking up a little bit on him; in my periphery I could see I was pulling ahead, and that encouraged me. From then on I was all out elbows and knees to the finish."

So many thoughts go through a runner's mind at this point in such a race. For an unheralded runner going one-on-one against a champion, they are often thoughts of doubt. Did I go out too fast? Has he just been playing with me all along? Will I collapse before the finish? How much do I have left? According to Ed, "Sometimes you get this horrible feeling that 'Oh no, I've kicked too early.' I was at full speed and still had a ways to go and I wondered if he goes to that other gear will I be able to hold him off. So now I'm hoping and waiting and recruiting every muscle in my body trying to get to the finish line before he does, and it's inching closer but it's not coming fast enough. I was tapped out at full speed and was beginning to fatigue at that point and in my mind I was thinking, 'I'm in trouble now,' but as we got ever closer to the line I remember just throwing my arms up in desperation and then I realized I hit the finishing tape before he did. In my running career that was the highest high I ever had, and I remember actually jumping up and down in the chute, not so much that I'd won, but that I had beat Wayne Pinto. I wasn't being obnoxious in my exuberance; it was just a real sincere happy feeling of accomplishment. Wayne was very gracious in defeat and congratulated me. I guess it wasn't as if I didn't have good credentials, but it was still a reach for me to try and run with that guy. It was a huge moment for me.

"There was a picture of me in the Provo *Daily Herald* in the finishing chute looking very tired and skinny. That race was the first time anyone became aware of me, the first time I appeared on anyone's radar, and from that point on my career was a lot different. Whenever I was at a big meet and found myself looking around and seeing guys who looked much faster and fitter and more capable than me, I would reflect back on that race against the best runner I ever faced. I would think, 'Wait a minute, I beat Wayne Pinto and Wayne Pinto can beat all of these guys, therefore I should be able to beat these guys too.' It just made me feel a lot more worthy going into competitions. It launched me forward to a successful campaign the rest of my high school career, which in turn set me up to get a track scholarship to Brigham Young University. After that, I was fortunate to have a long career at the highest level and had some great highs like winning NCAA championships and making the '88 and '92 Olympic teams. Looking back, those were all great, but I don't think the emotion and sheer joy I felt from any of those more public races was any higher than the high I had the day I beat Wayne Pinto."

Running Tip: "Sometimes it's good to put your goal out there a little bit. Don't be afraid to go for it. Set a goal and make it a goal that makes you stretch. Execute a plan and go with the plan, and occasionally get out of your comfort zone."

Dawna Stone

According to the winner of the 2005 edition of NBC's *The Apprentice: Martha Stewart*, the reality show experience was just like an endurance race. "It was about day to day or mile by mile. For me, no matter how hard it was, I knew I was going to wake up the next day and have another goal and just take it one step at a time until I reached the finish line." Looking back on her being chosen as Martha Stewart's apprentice, Dawna Stone says she was prepared for the rigors of that competition by her ability to reach another finish line earlier in her career; she just can't recall crossing it. "I have a picture to prove it, but I don't remember crossing the finish line. I don't remember my husband walking me to the medical tent, and I don't remember me leaving the medical tent."

The founder of *Women's Running* magazine and author of *Winning Nice* and *Healthy You!* was referring to her experience in the 1999 Ironman World Championship Triathlon in Hawaii. It was her best race, but not for reasons one would expect. As a hint to the outcome of that 2.4-mile swim, 112-mile bike ride, and 26.2-mile run, she says, "Everyone who knows me knows I don't give up, even maybe when I should." Already a runner and an accomplished swimmer, Dawna had the Ironman on her bucket list for quite a while. "I knew I could run and I knew I could swim, and how hard could biking be?" So Dawna hired a coach and committed a year of training to prepare for the race. "When I made it into the Ironman I was thrilled," she recalls, "more excited about it than I have ever been. My husband wasn't happy with how much training I was doing, so I knew this was probably going to be it for a while."

A week before the race, Dawna and her husband left for Hawaii. But after a stop on Oahu before the final flight to the Big Island, Dawna's odyssey began to go awry; it all started with a chicken sandwich. "After my husband and I left San Diego we had a layover at Honolulu airport," she says, "and I ordered a grilled chicken sandwich while we waited. I ate about half of it and realized the chicken was not cooked at all—they must have put some on the grill and pulled off the wrong one. So I stopped eating it and really didn't think anything more about it. We flew into Kona right before dinnertime and by then I wasn't feeling so great. I saw my coach and told him that my stomach was in knots and I felt sick, but he said I was just nervous, and that it was just excitement since it was my dream to be in Hawaii."

As it turned out, what Dawna had was much more than excitement and a nervous stomach. "That night I went to bed and woke up in the middle of the night throwing up blood. I've never been that sick in my entire life. My husband rushed me to the emergency room and I ended up having an extremely bad case of salmonella. They had to give me seven bags of IV fluid. Despite taking antinausea medication, Dawna had trouble holding any solid food down until three days before the race, when her body could tolerate some steamed rice. "The doctor told my husband that I definitely cannot race," she says, "but on race day I decided I didn't care what the doctor said. I had spent an entire year training for that race and I was going to do it. So I started the race."

Dawna had been a competitive swimmer and, despite her condition, had an excellent swim in that first leg of the Ironman. "I came out with the pros in under an hour on the swim. When I got on the bike I was still not feeling great, and about halfway through the course after the turnaround I started throwing up." Nevertheless, Dawna kept riding and managed to finish the bike leg with a fairly good time. It was then she had a decision to make: whether to abandon the race at that point, knowing she had done the best she could under the circumstances, or continue in that condition for another 26.2 miles to the finish. "I looked at my watch and I didn't know how I was going to keep going," she recalls. "But I didn't know if I was ever going to do that again either—another Ironman. I had a pretty fast swim and a pretty decent bike even though it wasn't as good as I usually do, so I just remembered thinking that I could walk the marathon and still make the seventeen-hour cutoff. I was pretty sick and it probably wasn't smart for me to keep going, but I figured even if I walk the entire marathon I'll still come in before the cutoff, and that's what I did.

"I started running a little bit, but I think because of the dehydration and cramping and throwing up during the bike segment my calves and quads were tightening up with each step. So I'd run a few steps and then walk. I think the biggest thing keeping me going was that I truly believed that it might be my one and only Ironman. I wanted to do it once. And I didn't want to finish one minute over the cutoff time either; I wanted to finish so I could legitimately say I did it. I didn't care if I had to crawl under that finish banner; I wasn't stopping. Never in my life have I been in more pain than I was in that marathon. I walked a very large portion of that marathon—most of it, but every time I'd see my husband and my mother-in-law along the course I tried to run a little because I knew my husband would pull me off if he saw me just walking, given that the doctor told him not to let me race."

Dawna doesn't remember much of the last part of the run, except for the many runners catching and passing her. "There might have been people walking at that point, but to be honest, I don't know if I could have had a conversation with anybody." And though she can't recall crossing the finish line, her time of fourteen and a half hours easily beat the cutoff. "I did spend a lot of time in the medical tent afterwards," she says, "and now that I know more about it I wouldn't let somebody else do what I did, but I'm not one to back down.

"I remember being so disappointed, feeling like, 'Why me?' I had worked so hard. Why did I have to get that chicken sandwich and why did I have to get sick? I was just really mad about the whole situation. But after a while I thought how fortunate I was to have been in a situation like that because now, no matter what happens in a race, it can never feel as bad as that day felt, so everything else seems pretty easy. It was probably one of the best things that ever happened to me in terms of sports because I know in most things I do I'll never feel that bad again."

Whether starting a magazine, writing a book, or competing against cutthroat contestants to become Martha Stewart's apprentice, Dawna embraces the lessons she learned from her Ironman experience. "In business, I always look back specifically to this endeavor," she says. "You can work extremely hard but you never know what's going to happen. You've just got to persevere. Whether you believe you can cross the finish line at the Ironman or if you truly believe that a new magazine is something you're going to love, you need to keep going forward. It's amazing what you can do both physically and mentally to get something done. There are going to be tough times in any part of a race or in any part of starting or growing a business, and it's all about having that perseverance. Now when I do speaking engagements, I tell people that whenever I have something difficult in my life happening, something that's painful either in sports or outside of sports, I think back and say, 'No way is this as painful as that day I was in Hawaii walking and running those twenty-six miles.' It makes everything to this day feel so much easier."

Running Tip: "If you have a goal, truly believe that you can make it happen and then you can. Just have that mental power over your mind to accomplish something. Set your goals high and you'll be amazed at what your mind can do for you, and you'll be amazed at what your body can do for you."

Weldon Johnson

Five runners had split from the rest of the field with a mile to go in the 10K National Championship at Stanford University. The first four, Alan Culpepper, Meb Keflezighi, Abdi Abdirahman, and Dan Brown, shared NCAA championships, cross-country titles, and Olympic team credentials. The fifth runner, Weldon Johnson, never even earned All-America status in college. So if you have to ask, "What's wrong this picture?" it's understandable. After all, those were Weldon Johnson's very words too. But although he wasn't a big name in running circles, Weldon was doing something many of us never do: when it counted most, he was giving himself a chance.

Most runners know the popular website LetsRun.com better than they do the twin brothers who created it, Weldon ("Wejo") and Robert ("Rojo") Johnson. The site, with its two primary goals of covering running as a professional sport and helping more people get more out of their running, receives a million unique visitors each month. "I quit my job to train for the Olympic Marathon Trials in 2000," says Weldon, "and I thought, 'What am I going to do with my free time when I'm not running?' The Internet was new and there wasn't a site for the more serious runner, but the beauty of the Internet is that you can cater to a niche audience. So my twin brother and I started it. At the beginning we just plastered 'LetsRun.com' on my racing singlet. Soon we really hit it off with those in elite running circles. There was a little luck involved, some word of mouth, some of it was by accident, some of it was just good timing, and then a lot of hard work. I didn't think thirteen years later we would still be doing it."

At Weldon's first track meet after moving to Flagstaff, Arizona for training, he lowered his personal best 10K time from 29:49 to 28:27. "That's a huge jump especially at that level," says Weldon. "So then people were saying, 'Who the hell is this guy?' When the marathon trials rolled around and *USA Today* had me as one of ten guys to watch, I thought, 'What the hell's going on here?'" Weldon placed twenty-fifth in that marathon, but the progress he saw in his running encouraged him to see just how far he could go. "When training went really well in 2000 I thought I could be top ten in the country," he says. "And if you're at that level you have to think you can be in the top three. In my whole life I wanted to be at this level, and I thought that maybe I should continue to pursue this." His outlook didn't change after he had an encouraging fourth place in the 2001 USA 10K Championship. "I just got fourth in the nationals and the running was going too well. I could do the other things (like business school) later," he says. "As a kid you dream of going to the Olympics, so why wouldn't I pursue that?"

Although the website was running smoothly, Weldon's training began hitting some bumps in the road. The 2003 10K National Championship would be the next major test in terms of establishing himself as Olympic material, but his first 10K of 2003 was only "borderline" in terms of qualifying him for that meet. Weldon, however, didn't let a mediocre time affect his outlook. "Basically I put my life on hold for three years," he says. "Going into 2003 I had been hurt, my training wasn't going well, and then I had to drop out of the race leading up to the national championship. But I didn't quit my job and dedicate the previous three years of my life *not* to do anything in that race. On paper, sure, it was crazy to think I was going to do anything well, but that's one of the reasons it makes this my proudest race."

Before, Weldon thought everything had to go perfectly in training in order for someone to perform at their best in a race. "I would psych myself out in races," he says. "I thought the top guys always ran well because they did these great workouts, but I found that's not always the case. All you can do anytime you race is to give your best effort. My mindset in that race was to just give myself a chance. I had quit my job, and this race was my opportunity—why *not* go for it? I think a lot of times in my career I put artificial limits on what was possible. Back in college when I wasn't that good, I would think about what time I should run a certain race, or ask the coach at what pace I should run. If I started out wanting to run twenty-nine minutes, for example, I wouldn't have a chance of winning. But I've shown I can run with the best and that's what I was trying to do. At one level I thought maybe this could be a disaster. Maybe I was crazy to think I could run with them, but then I would be limiting myself again. I was at that race to really put myself in it—I wasn't there just to run my best time. Everyone can't be Rocky, but occasionally it happens."

Weldon went out near the front for the first mile to be in the right mindset for competing at such a high level. Gradually he began drifting back as other runners began to pass. "I remember thinking that I've got to be careful," he says. "Those times when everybody's hurting and the line breaks in front of you, it becomes easier to think you're too far back, and soon it's over. I said to myself, 'This is it, what are you doing? You have to get back up there and give it another chance, man!' So I pushed my way back to the front group again. Once I put myself back up there I was pretty competitive and I was in it.

"The hardest part is in the middle, just getting through miles. I was up there the first mile and settled back in the second mile, then got back up there again in mile three. After that it's just about hanging on until you get to the last mile and then it's all about competing. With a mile to go, it was Meb, Abdi, Alan Culpepper, and Dan Brown. Those guys and me—I felt like Forrest Gump. I shouldn't be up there, right? My brother and other friends were there and I was well aware of other people who were cheering for me. So all of a sudden I did the 'raise the roof' sign with my hands to pump up the crowd. I wasn't arrogant about it. I was just thinking, 'This is awesome.' I was aware of how well I was doing and I was enjoying it. Being up there was what I had dreamed about, what I've wanted after all the thousands of hours of training. I thought, 'This is fun. Let's not take it too seriously."'

Meb Keflezighi suddenly took off and only Alan Culpepper could follow. "My only regret in the race is that I wanted to be up with Meb," he recalls. "In some ways it's crazy; there's no way I'm going to beat Meb Keflezhigi, but when I say that I'm limiting myself again. I may not have been able to beat him but I could have gone to the front." Alan Culpepper eventually caught and passed Meb to win, with Dan Brown finishing third. In a national championship, the top three finishers automatically qualify for the World Championships, and fourth place gets an invitation to the Pan American Games. "One thing I'm proud about is that I was in fifth place coming down the last stretch with Abdi in front of me, but I was gaining on him. Right before the finish line he lets up, and I went by him, which got me on the Pam America Games team. I can always say I beat Abdi Abdirahman." Weldon's time of 28:06 was a personal best by four seconds.

"That was the culmination of what I had learned about myself in my running career," says Weldon. "Running taught me that the body is an amazing thing, and I've learned I can do a lot more than what I thought was possible. I can run 4:30 per mile back-to-back for six miles, and I think, 'How?' Even in training I wasn't close to that. I think it helped that I wasn't that great in high school or college. I wanted to get better because I just loved running. I learned that two things determine how well we do: what is your absolute maximum, and how close can you come to that on the day it matters? My emphasis was on the latter. You may not be the best guy, but if you are as good as you can be when it matters, you'll do pretty well. A lot of it is just running best when it counts, and that's how it happened in that race. I was able to put it together on the day it mattered most, and I did about as well as I was going to do. I'm proud that I gave myself that chance."

Running Tip: "On the day of the race, don't limit yourself. Negative thoughts don't help. Give yourself a chance and believe in yourself. All you can do is the best you can."

Marla Runyan

"I had a really bad attitude going in that I would finish fourth," recalls Marla Runyan of her race at the 2002 Prefontaine Classic. The 3,000 meters was a distance at which she always struggled, and considering the stiff competition, she was not at all confident about her chances. Marla hung tough for the first half of the race before the three favorites opened up a gap on the field. But then one small voice broke through the din of 10,000 screaming fans and changed everything. Marla Runyan may be legally blind, but there was nothing wrong with her hearing that day at Oregon's Hayward Field.

When Marla's vision began deteriorating at age nine, it took a retina specialist to finally determine the cause. The diagnosis was Stargardt's Disease, a form of macular degeneration. "My vision acuity is 20/300 in the left and 20/200 in the right," she says, which means Marla has to be twenty feet from an object to see it with the same degree of clarity as a normally sighted person can from 200 feet. "So by definition I'm legally blind. I was a very slow reader because I couldn't see what I was reading half the time, and school was always hard for me, but when I went out for recess I would just take off and run. Running was a way for me to visualize my world. I couldn't see what was in the distance, but if I ran there then I could get closer to it and see it. So I would run to one side of the playground and see what was there, then run to the other side and put all those pieces together, then I'd memorize all those things."

On the soccer field, Marla used a similar strategy. "I would just cover the entire field because that was the only way I could keep track of the ball, so I was constantly running." After years of running on playgrounds and soccer fields, it was only natural that Marla would gravitate to the track in high school and later at San Diego State. In college she established herself as a serious competitor in the heptathlon and sprint races, and enjoyed gold-medal success at the 1992 Paralympic Games in Barcelona. Her inspiring story continued when she became the first legally blind athlete to compete in the Olympics, where she finished 8th in the 1,500 meters in Sydney.

Two years later at the time of the Prefontaine Classic, Marla and her husband/coach were living in Eugene, and Hayward Field served as her home track. "I entered the 3,000 because my other events weren't being run at the meet," she says. "I was originally a 1,500 runner and had moved up to the 5,000 (5K), but was never comfortable in the 3,000. You can't really run 5K pace because that would be too slow. You need to run somewhere in between the 1,500 pace and the 5K pace, which is out of my comfort zone. I think of the 3,000 as a really long mile, but when the gun goes off you have seven and a half laps of it rather than four. So my whole attitude in the warm-up area was that I really hated that race."

Marla's main competition would be Ireland's Sonia O'Sullivan, who won the silver in the 5,000 meters in Sydney, and two Ethiopian runners. "I was confident that I could probably beat the other Americans in the race," she recalls, "but I didn't feel confident I could beat Sonia or the two Africans, one of whom had beat me the week before in a 5K. The gun went off and Sonia took it out hard. She just went right to the lead and pressed really hard. I was in the middle of the pack and stayed there." Eventually, just as Marla expected, Sonia and the two Africans began to pull away and a gap formed between them and the rest of the field. It is a situation that presents one of her biggest challenges. "I can see the track and where my feet are striking the track and the lines on the track, and I can see when other runners are near me, but if there's a gap, if they get away, they seem very far away to me. Beyond that I can't tell if it's one runner or two runners. I see the movement ahead of me, but I can't tell who they are and how many there are."

By necessity, Marla had found a way to deal with that problem at some of her track meets. "I use the track announcer," she says. "The announcer is always saying where the runners are on the track, who is up front, and the names of the runners ahead of me. Sometimes he will even call out our splits. I used any information I could get. I don't think they even know that I needed the help. At the Prefontaine meet I could see movement up ahead and the announcer called out their names, so that's how I knew there were three and not four." With every lap, however, fourth place was looking more and more like the best finish Marla could expect under the circumstances.

"With two laps to go I was coming down the homestretch thinking how much I hated that 3000-meter distance when I heard this little girl's voice from the crowd say, 'Come on Marla, you can do it!' It was so odd in a crowd of so many thousands of people that I could hear that one girl's voice. And as soon as I heard that little girl, there was an instantaneous reaction in my head. I was thinking, 'What are you doing, Marla? This is my track, this is my hometown, get in the race!' It was almost like I had been conceding the race. Then everything about my running changed."

At that point in the race, Marla was in 6th or 7th place, she wasn't exactly sure. But it was that gap between the three leaders and the rest of the field that was most critical. "I figured I had to have a plan," says Marla. "I had to get in contact with those three runners before the final lap. My plan was to gradually regain contact but still have something left at the end. So as soon as I heard that girl's voice I immediately got up to where I was leading the second pack and then spent the whole next lap pulling forward. I think with 600 meters to go I was about three strides from making contact with the two Africans, but Sonia was still leading. I knew the two Africans didn't have the kind of finishing speed that I had, and I had to get around them with one lap to go because I knew Sonia was going to really take off in that last lap. So off of the turn I was finally able to make contact, and right when the bell sounded for the final lap I passed them." From then on it would be a two-person race.

Just as Marla passed the two African runners, Sonia O'Sullivan began her kick, and Marla had no choice but to go with her. "I came up right behind Sonia, but she still had a good stride on me. As we went down the backstretch I could feel I was actually gaining on her, and as we came into the last turn I pulled up so close to her that her spike came up and nicked my right shin. We came off the final turn and I went out wide, and with 100 meters to go we both started our kicks. The whole crowd was cheering."

Of course, for a legally blind runner, there was one more challenge to overcome, and a fairly important one at that: locating the finish line. "From 100 meters away I can't see the finish," says Marla. "As I mentioned before, when I get closer to something I'm able to see it; it just comes into view for me a lot later than for anyone else. I am able to see the actual physical line, but I need to be no more than five meters away from it. But there are always a lot of other objects near the line like timers or a structure of some kind that are easier to pick up. So I see all the things you associate with a finish line area more than the white line on the track itself.

"I thought we were evenly matched at that point. I didn't know if I could go any faster, and I didn't feel she could go any faster. Then I remembered something from competing at the Pan Am Games—no matter how hard it is to hold back, if you have anything left you should wait until right before the finish line. Pulling ahead with fifty meters to go isn't going to help you if you can't hold onto it. So we ran side by side and literally at twenty meters I pulled ahead of her and won." The winning margin was forty-two hundredths of a second, and for Marla it was a personal best at that distance by five seconds.

"That was my best race because of how I was able to change my attitude and how significant that was in changing how I ran the race. You may not realize it, but your thinking in a race, whether positive or negative, can really affect your pace. If you go into a race and you're negative like I was, and you think, 'Oh, I have three more of these laps to go,' you're going to slow down. It's always how you perceive it. Instead you have to think,

'Okay, there are only three laps to go, I can do this.' I hated that distance and my confidence was low from losing a 5K the week before, so I underestimated what I was capable of. Yet I was able to salvage the race and win it, which is why I think it was so significant hearing that little girl's voice. Plus, I have a pleaser personality; I never want to disappoint anybody. In my running career I always felt such a strong obligation to my sponsors and to my agent, and I am always more concerned about disappointing them and other people than I am myself. Hearing that girl is when it occurred to me that I was disappointing someone by my negative attitude; I was disappointing that girl.

"So even though I qualified for and ran in two Olympics, the 3,000 meters at the Prefontaine meet is a very special race to me for those reasons. It's funny, isn't it? If I hadn't heard that little girl I think it would have been a whole different story."

Running Tip: "You have to be realistic of what you're capable of running, meaning you need to have the fitness for the race that's in front of you. I hear about people getting off the couch and saying they want to run a marathon. Well, why not start with a mile first? If you try to run a race that you're not trained to run, it will be miserable. The best race is usually the one that feels good. It doesn't necessarily hurt like at other times. And the reason it feels so good is that you were able to use the fitness you had."

Dick Beardsley

Dick Beardsley should have trusted his instincts rather than the hometown hero who was sharing the pace during the 1981 Grandma's Marathon. "He told me, 'It's your race, I'm just here to help you,'" says Dick, "but my first thought was that this guy is really just setting me up for the kill." Dick Beardsley and Garry Bjorklund ran side by side for most of those 26.2 miles until Dick took his eyes off the wily veteran. His struggle to catch up, take the lead, and survive a collision with a spectator made for a memorable race. What made it his *best* race, however, were the two people waiting for him at the finish line.

Just a few years earlier Dick had no idea he would become one of the top marathoners in US history. Although he ran in college, he had no plans after graduation except to return to the family dairy farm with his degree in agriculture. Still, he kept running, and an encouraging result in his first-ever marathon caused him to reconsider his future. "I thought, gosh, I could milk cows when I'm thirty, forty, or fifty," he recalls, "but I'll never again have the chance of seeing how good a runner I can become." So the Minnesota farm boy left the cows behind, took a one-room apartment in the big city (Minneapolis), and began to train full-time. Of course, not everyone was thrilled about this turn of events. "My dad thought I was the biggest fool that ever walked the earth."

New Balance thought otherwise. The running-shoe company became Dick's sponsor after a few more noteworthy performances, enabling him to continue running full-time. And by the time Joe Squires of the Greater Boston Track Club became his coach, Dick was in the midst of a streak that would put him in the *Guinness Book of World Records* as the only man to run thirteen consecutive personal bests in the marathon. One of those races was the inaugural London Marathon, which Dick won in a time of 2:11:48. Grandma's Marathon in Duluth, Minnesota was next on his agenda. "It was an exciting time for me," says Dick. "I had just won in London and there was a lot of publicity surrounding Grandma's Marathon because another Minnesota runner, Garry Bjorklund, was invited. He was the previous year's winner and the course record holder. The TV stations were promoting this big matchup between me, the young buck, and Garry, the seasoned veteran."

Leading up to the race, Dick was running 130-140 miles a week following a training program designed by his coach back in Boston. But twelve days before Grandma's Marathon, Dick designed his own workout. "I did a twenty-one-mile long run with two fast five-mile segments in under twenty-five minutes each," he recalls, "and two 'slower' five-mile segments at 5:20 pace. The last mile I went all out and ran in 4:36. When I called my coach and told him how my workout went, he started screaming at me on the phone. He was so afraid I would have nothing left for the race, but I felt like I was really ready to go."

Dick remembers it being one of those perfect days for a long distance race: cloudy and 48 degrees, with a bit of fog rolling in off Lake Superior. "The gun went off and right away Garry and I went out together. After about a half mile down the road with no one else in sight Garry turned to me and said, 'Just you and me, buddy. Whatever I can do to help you, that's what I'm here for.'" But Dick wasn't so sure. "This guy's a record holder," he says. "He's a Minnesota icon and an Olympian. And he was telling me it's *my* race?"

Nevertheless, Garry *was* helpful. That is, at first. "At about four and a half miles I got a terrible cramp in my side, and I wondered if I should say anything to Garry. Finally I told him and he said, 'No problem, we'll just back off the pace a little bit and we'll get a drink of water for you at the next aid station.' We did and the cramp went away." Next, Dick was given a lesson on running the tangents (the imaginary straight line from one curve to the next) in a road race. "I was running straight down the middle of the road and I noticed Garry was always running off to the side and cutting the corners. Finally after seven miles he came over to me said, 'What the heck are you doing running right down the middle of the road all the time?' Well you're cutting every corner, I said, and that's cheating! He said, 'Dick, when they measure a marathon course they measure it by the tangents, so you're running a lot further than you need to.' We continued running a sub five-minute pace side by side, following the tangents, and when we came to the halfway point he turned to me and said, 'You're on pace for a 2:09!'"

With his veteran rival giving him advice and pacing him to what would be his fastest marathon ever, Dick let his guard down. "I had a terrible habit back then," he recalls. "Even if I had a lead or if I knew there was nobody near me, I liked to look back over my shoulder. So just before the Duluth city limits where the crowd starts getting big, I turned to look behind me, and when I turned back around Garry was about fifty meters ahead of me and just flying. I thought, 'Son of a gun, he set me up!' He waited until we got into the town where the crowd gets big and the hometown people were going to get behind him."

Dick didn't panic. Because of his training, he knew he could throw in a pretty good surge when needed, just like on that last long training run leading up to the race. After another mile he caught up to Garry, but felt he needed to make a statement. "I remember thinking that I had to take care of him then, so I threw down the hammer and put in another hard surge." At the twenty-mile mark a volunteer on a bike rode up to me and told me I had just run a 4:40 mile, but that Garry was still right behind me. So I picked it up even more and at mile twenty-one the volunteer came up to me and said that I had just run a 4:36 mile, and that Garry was hurting. I thought if I didn't back off then, I'd be hurting too." Then at the series of double hills called Lemon Drop Hill, Dick's cramp returned. "If I didn't get rid of that cramp the whole field would catch me," he says. "I was doing everything I could—blowing through pursed lips, rubbing my side—nothing was helping. But I knew this: if I could just get to the last mile—I didn't care if my legs were coming apart—I could get to the finish line. I knew that at the Radisson hotel there was one mile to go in the race. So I was still running with the cramp when I finally saw the outline of the Radisson and I knew as soon as I made that left turn there was just one more mile."

But then Dick saw the outline of someone up ahead who was perhaps even more threatening than his fading rival. "The crowd was thick along one side of the street with traffic on the other, and I noticed a little kid playing with a toy truck in the narrow corner of the street where I had to make the turn. I thought surely mom and dad were going to get that kid out of the way, but I was fifty meters away and the boy was still there. Finally the boy picked up his toy and began walking off the course, but all of a sudden he saw me and just froze. Forty meters away, then thirty. What do I do? If I went right there was a lane of traffic and if I went left there was a crowd of people and a lamppost." And if Dick pulled up he risked injury. "It was either get hit by a car or run into the crowd or the lamppost." Or else he could take the path of least resistance. "I realized then that the only moveable object was that kid, so I ran smack dab into him and he went flying into the crowd. I looked back over my shoulder and saw he was crying, but at least he was still breathing … and it made my cramp go away!

"Now I had my stride back but I had no idea how fast I was running. When I came around the last corner there must have been 30,000 people lining both sides of the street and they were going crazy. Some people in the crowd yelled that I was going to break 2:10 and I didn't believe it. When I got a little closer I could see the clock ahead reading '2:09 something' and my first thought was they forgot to start it! When I came across the finish line the clock read 2:09:36 and I jumped up and down like a little kid who just found a train set under the Christmas tree.

"Yeah, beating Garry Bjorklund was big, and winning Grandma's was big, but it was my best race because my mom and dad were there at the finish line to see me. It was the first time they ever saw me run a marathon. You could hit my dad over the head with a two-by-four and he wouldn't cry, but he was crying then. I get choked up just talking about it. My mom and dad were both crying and my dad was hugging me and wiping away his tears and I was just overwhelmed with emotion. Years earlier when I told my dad I was going to run full-time instead of staying on the farm and milking cows, he thought I was nuts. But eventually when he saw the dedication I had, he became my biggest supporter. He and my mom at that finish line; that was really special."

Running Tip: "No matter the level of your abilities, in every race you are going to be a little uncomfortable physically. Just focus on the next mile. If you break it down like that, it makes a world of difference." Dick is a motivational speaker and founder of the Dick Beardsley Foundation, an organization that promotes education and greater openness about chemical dependency, and helps sufferers defray the cost of treatment.

Keith Brantly

"He did it to me the same way every time," says Keith Brantly. "I'd go out and he'd sit on me. I'd make a surge in the middle of the race and try to drop him, but couldn't. And then he would outsprint me at the end." The frustrated future Olympian would have one more shot at his rival at the Florida High School Cross-Country State Championship, though he would probably have to run the perfect race to beat him. But is there such a thing as the perfect race? Ask Keith Brantly.

According to the seven-time US National Road Racing Champion and Olympic marathoner, "Most runners will tell you that it is difficult to say a race they ran was perfect in every way. They would dissect it, analyze it, tear it apart, and say they could have done this or that better; it's human nature never to be satisfied. When I think about every race I've run, the only one I executed exactly how I was supposed to, before the start and during the race, and with everything else coming together perfectly, was the Florida High School Cross-Country State Championship. I did exactly as my coach had prescribed, but it wasn't an easy task."

The plan that his coach prescribed was for Keith to go out fast, completely surprise his rival, and teach him a lesson. Or as Keith bluntly puts it, "We wanted to take this kid out to the woodshed and beat him senseless. We based the plan on the fact that there were few strategies available to us; he was one of the best runners not just in Florida but in the nation. We felt that this was a time to take a chance and that it was worth taking the risk. It had to be a shocking, audacious move, something he didn't expect. There was no way I was going to beat him otherwise."

To challenge Keith mentally as well as physically for the event, his coach at Winter Haven High School prescribed one particular workout of 12 x 400 repeats (one 400-meter lap repeated 12 times) at a 70-second pace per lap. After each lap he would come to a complete stop for 15 seconds. "Typically we take a minute rest between each one," says Keith, "but when you do only a 15-second rest it really challenges you. By the time I decelerated to a stop, it was time to turn around for the next one. My coach called it 'aerobic 400s.' I just called it pain. We had done some other things in training that really prepared our team for the meet, including some pretty fast interval workouts, so I felt like I was ready to go out hard. I knew what I could do, but we really weren't sure what it would do to my rival." Looking back on that situation, Keith recalls some advice he once received from the great British runner Sebastian Coe. "He told me the idea of a tactic is that it does more damage to your competitor than it does to you."

As he waited before the start of the 3-mile race, which was held on a grassy and partly sandy course alongside an airport, Keith wasn't exactly calm. "We had to do something that was least expected, had the biggest risk, and had the least chance for a positive outcome; I was scared to death. But when the gun went off I knew what I had to do. I had to run up a huge lead on that guy and just try to maintain and do the best I could. I had to believe what my coach was telling me and execute. And that's what I did.

"I went out at 4:25 for the first mile and the other guy didn't respond because he probably thought I was going to come back. I was about 50 yards ahead at the time and I don't think anyone really expected that." Keith wasn't used to being the front-runner, especially one with such a big lead. "They probably thought I was out of my mind and that it was not going to be hard to catch me," he says. "I got through the first two miles running mainly out of fear. I was afraid to look back. It's riskier to go out hard because you don't have the element of being the hunter and you don't have the advantage of drafting.

I thought it would be craziness to go out like that, but I didn't think I had much of a choice."

Keith's coach could see how their audacious plan played out from a vantage point a half mile before the finish. "I'll never forget the look on my coach's face," says Keith. "I almost thought he was having a heart attack because he was grabbing his chest and had this pained look on his face. All I heard him say was, 'You've got him. You've got him. Don't let up.' That's when I looked back and didn't see anyone. It actually made me relax, so I could run harder because I didn't have to be concerned with holding anybody off. When you see pictures of the race, the others weren't even in the shot.

"I remember crossing the finish line and feeling somewhat refreshed. I didn't feel physically exhausted, I was more mentally exhausted. I think what took it out of me was the stress that I had to execute on a strategy that we had never before tried. And for it to work, the other guy had to play his part. If he had had an exceptional day, it would have been a different race. Still, even after getting beaten by him a couple times during the season, I never felt it was beyond the realm of possibility that, if I had a good day, I could beat him, and that makes a big difference.

"He and I chatted a little after the race and I could tell he had a real attitude of resignation. Not anger or disappointment, just resignation that there was nothing he could have done. It's very temping for me to name my Olympic qualifying marathon as my best race," says Keith, "but we're always looking for that matchup of being able to influence other runners mentally by what we can do physically like I did in this race. We don't get that very often. My coach knew that if I did these certain things and performed them well in the race, I would be able to effect a change in my opponent's head."

In the movie *The Endless Summer*, two surfers circle the globe in search of the perfect wave, a quest Keith Brantly knows all too well from spending countless hours in the surf during his youth. "You can sit out there all day long and hope the perfect wave is right around the corner, but in reality it isn't. But I can say that the Cross-Country State Championship was as close to the perfect race as I'll ever get. When I try to take it apart I can't find anything I did wrong. And not just from an execution standpoint; the whole scenario went my way. I just think it was one of those days where training and strategy and action came together for me, and everything else played out as well. Physically I was able to back it up, and to have all those stars aligned, well, you just don't get that very often."

Running Tip: "It's important for every runner, whether elite or recreational, to understand that training is only half the process for improving your performance. The other half is allowing your body to recover and adapt from the hard training. The body will always adapt to stress eventually."

Jennipher Walters

On January 10, 2010, the morning of the Disney Marathon, Florida's orange crop was frozen. So was Jenn Walters. "I read up on which courses were good for beginners, which ones were fairly flat, and which ones had temperatures that weren't extreme one way or the other," she says. "The Disney Marathon seemed perfect, plus it seemed so kid-like to go to Disney World! So I was thinking it was going to be sixty-five degrees and sunny, but when the race started, it was in the twenties." Unfortunately, the miserable weather was an omen for Jenn's first marathon. She would definitely need a cheerleader to help her get through it; fortunately, she found one.

Like many distance runners, Jenn was intrigued by the challenge of running 26.2 miles. "In high school I hated running," she recalls, "but in college I got bit by the addiction of running farther and farther each time." After completing a 5K and then a 10K race, she felt ready for even longer distances. "I ran a few half marathons but I wanted to be challenged even more, so a marathon was put on my fitness bucket list. It's like street cred. When people hear that I've run a marathon they say, 'Oh, you're really committed. You *really* run!'"

It was also in college where Jenn was bitten by the fitness bug after joining a group exercise class. As with her running, she took that interest to the next level by becoming an AFAA-certified group exercise instructor and a certified personal trainer. "I really liked teaching and sharing advice with others," she says. Along with a degree in health journalism, it seemed only natural that Jenn would find a career dispensing fitness information and counseling to women. In 2008, because "we didn't think women were getting the full empowering, fitness-can-be-fun message," Jenn co-founded the website FitBottomedGirls.com. The site, which recently celebrated its fifth year of "keeping a lid on the junk in the trunk," receives 65,000 unique visitors a week and has over 100,000 Facebook fans and Twitter followers.

Because she wanted a running companion for that first ever 26.2-mile run, Jenn had to convince someone else that the Disney Marathon could be empowering and fun. Tish Merritt, Jenn's best friend and a contributor to the website, finally said "yes," and they drew up a training schedule to follow even though they lived in different states. "I was really dedicated," says Jenn. "I rarely missed a training run. All of my training runs felt really good and I paid a lot of attention to my nutrition and recovery. I finally did a long run of 20 miles and it felt really good." Tish, however, was having her doubts. "She was in an area where she couldn't run outside, so she did all her workouts on the treadmill. She was worried if that was going to be enough training for racing outdoors." As it turned out, Tish had nothing to worry about.

"We had no time goals," says Jenn about the race. "We just wanted to finish and enjoy the experience. The race started at the crack of dawn and we were miserable. I couldn't feel anything on my body for the first six miles because it was so cold. Even the water at the aid stations was frozen!" Eventually they both warmed up, but along with the thaw came the pain. "Around mile seven my left hip and leg started to hurt really bad." Jenn had suffered a previous bout with hip pain at the end of her training, but thought the downtime leading up to the race would help her recover. "At first I didn't tell Tish about my problem because she was having the best running day of her life. She said she felt like she could run all day." But when the pain became too much to bear at mile twelve, Jenn could keep quiet no longer.

"I told Tish and she said, 'Well, just tell me when you want to stop, we'll take as many walk breaks as you want, and we'll do whatever you need.' She would say, 'Let's run up to the top of this overpass and then we'll walk a little bit.' At mile twenty it was so painful I really just wanted it to be over, and if Tish had not been there, I would have been one of the runners you see standing alone on the side of the road crying. She did so much for addressing the mental side of things. And I remember her saying, 'Focus. Is there anything on your body that *doesn't* hurt right now? Then let's just focus on that!' Sometimes you need a cheerleader, sometimes you need that same person to be quiet, and at other times you just need someone to say, 'Okay this sucks right now but we're going to do this.' Tish was a good mix of all that."

Jenn and Tish agreed that once they reached mile twenty-six near Epcot Center, they would run as fast as they could to the finish because the pain would then be over. "I took off at the mile marker running for the finish," says Jenn, "and I looked back and Tish was still there; she hadn't noticed the mile marker. But she came sprinting up in time for us to hold hands and cross the finish line together. Then we both immediately started crying. After crossing that line I felt like I was experiencing every single emotion one could have all at once. Whenever times were tough during a training run, I'd always think of crossing the finish line and imagine what that moment would be like and how proud I would feel."

The irony wasn't lost on Jenn as she recounts the reasons the Disney Marathon was her best race. "My training went well and her training didn't go well, but I was the one who got hurt during the race and she got me through it. Tish was having one of those days when you just feel fantastic and she could have been ticked off at me because she could have achieved a much better time in her first marathon, but that's not what she did. She was there for me, she stayed with me, and she was my cheerleader. It was by far my biggest running accomplishment, especially because we did it together."

Running Tip: "Grab a running buddy or soul mate to accompany you in a race or long training run. Someone who knows you really well and knows when to push and when to lay off. Someone who will just be there for you."

Brian Sell

The runner who once thought he wasn't good enough was actually having a pretty good day. By the halfway point on the hilly Central Park marathon course he was among an elite group chasing the leaders. By mile eighteen, while the others were content to hold their positions, he threw in a surge. With five miles to go he was alone in third place and pressed his advantage over those now chasing him. And when he cruised up the final hills to secure that third-place position behind Ryan Hall and Dathan Ritzenhein, he also secured a spot on the 2008 US Olympic Marathon team. Most would assume that performance at the Olympic Trials, which he calls "a career pinnacle," was his best ever. But if you ask Brian Sell, his best performance actually came eight years earlier and five hundred miles away on a hilly golf course in Ann Arbor, Michigan. On that day, the team's success meant more to him than individual glory, which is why it was, and still is, his best race.

"St. Francis? Where the hell is St. Francis?" That was the question Brian Sell and his teammates were often asked when competing at regional cross-country meets against schools out of their conference. His tiny college of two thousand in the tiny town of Loretto, Pennsylvania was the perennial underdog among the running powerhouses at those away meets. "We'd race all these big schools with numerous All-Americans," he says. "It was like David versus Goliath." Of course, the ragtag outfits his team wore only added to that underdog perception. "You would see a lot of those teams warming up in perfectly matching brand new Nike uniforms, and we would be wearing basic gray sweatpants with maybe a white jacket, or red wind pants with a different-colored pullover; we viewed ourselves as the *Bad News Bears* of cross-country." Then came the wisecracks. "They would say, 'They don't even have matching uniforms so they can't be very good.' We heard those comments and took them to heart, and always raced with a chip on our shoulder."

Brian Sell found himself among the Davids and not the Goliaths because he was a late bloomer. His first love in high school was wrestling; running long and hard was just a way to stay lean and mean for competition on the mat. But on a whim he decided to try out for the track team after wrestling season, and quickly emerged as the team's top distance runner. Though he excelled on the track that year, Brian admits the caliber of competition in his district was not very formidable, and his stellar achievements flew under the radar of college coaches. When no recruiters came calling, he enrolled at Messiah College and decided to focus on his studies rather than track. "Honestly, I just didn't think I was good enough." Still, his desire for competition and his passion for the sport never waned ("It's always a good day when I get a run in."), so the following year he joined the cross-country team and began to lay the foundation for the Olympic-caliber athlete he was to become.

Of course, one thing he didn't count on becoming was homesick; too many exits on the Pennsylvania Turnpike away from family and friends. But in retrospect, maybe that wasn't such a bad thing after all. Indeed, it wasn't until Brian transferred to St. Francis to be closer to home that he began to blossom as a college runner. The hills had something to do with it. "You can't go half a mile on campus without going up or down a hill," he says, "so we became really good on hills across the board." The golf course on which the St. Francis cross-country team trained and competed began with a screaming downhill followed by an excruciating uphill. Weekly training sessions included 500-meter repeats on those hills and 4 x 1 mile repeats on the track at 5-minute pace, with total weekly mileage topping out near triple digits.

By his senior year, Brian was posting some pretty good numbers for a small college runner—or *any* runner for that matter. His eye-opening times of twenty-five minutes and change on the demanding 8K (4.9 miles) course meant he no longer flew under the radar of rival coaches. More importantly, those consistent results empowered him with the confidence he once lacked. "I knew I could probably run in the low 25s just about anywhere if I could do it at St. Francis." But even with those fast times, it was the friendship and camaraderie of the team that held the most meaning for him. "The St. Francis cross-country team was by far the best team I've ever been on as far as a combination of teammates who were also close friends. We would push each other, but always leave it on the field. Then we would go to a party all together on the weekend and have a good time." Nowhere else was that combination of speed and team unity more evident than at the University of Michigan Wolverine Inter-regional 8K on October 15, 2000.

"Most of our trips were not overnight, so this was a big event for us as a team, the biggest of the season." And what did that close-knit band of small-school runners do their first night on a major college campus? "We sneaked into the Big House (Michigan's football stadium) and did wind sprints across the field. But, you know, we did them all as a team." Warming up the next morning in their typical mismatched outfits, the team looked around at some of the giants of college track: Florida, Texas, UCLA, Washington, Michigan, Tennessee. Nevertheless, his team remained confident from a hard season of training. "Who knew when we would see this level of competition again," he recalls. "It was all or nothing. We just wanted to give it our best effort."

A unique scoring format makes cross-country arguably the ultimate team sport. Points are awarded to individual runners equal to the position in which they finish, which are then compiled into a team score. The team with the lowest score wins the meet. At the Wolverine Inter-regional, the fastest five finishers out of eight team members counted towards that team score. Therefore, one team's non-scoring sixth-place runner could still aim to finish ahead of another team's fifth runner in order to "displace" that competitor farther down in the finishing order. It was just that strategy that helped St. Francis. "Each teammate worked hard that day no matter how little a part they played in the team score," says Brian. "It was an 'all for one' kind of thing. Our sixth man knew he wasn't going to score but still ran a personal best.

"Standing at the starting line that day, I knew I could be pretty competitive and I wanted to give it all the effort I could. There had been a few races in the past where I had given up, and I regretted it every time." During the race, the hilly course layout played to his strength. "I remember there were several short, steep hills that I was able to churn up easily. My coach had filled us in on the big "players" that day, and I tried to keep the top three or four guys in sight the whole time. The plan for me was to try and make a move at four miles if I was able, and that plan worked pretty well. With a mile to go I was still right up there with the leaders, so I felt pretty confident and was able to run a decent time in the end." Of course, Brian's time was more than just "decent." His 24:53 was good enough for second place overall! More important to him, however, is recalling how his teammates did. "The big thing for me was turning around after I crossed the line to see my teammates coming in all packed together, and I did some quick math to figure out where we might have finished. Texas finished first that day, but the moment they started writing that "S" for St. Francis on the scoreboard in second place, we were pretty fired up. It was pretty cool to see our name ahead of all those big schools.

"Sure, individually, the Olympic Trials marathon is probably the biggest race of my life," he says. "But a lot of little memories make this race the best in my mind. It was just a good combination of me running well and the team running well. I did well as an individual, but there were seven guys enjoying the day along with me. That's what made it the best."

Running Tip: "Give 100% effort no matter what. You'll feel a lot better if you do, and you never know what the outcome may be at the end. There have been a few races where I have given up and I regretted it every time."

Allen Leigh

Most people in Allen Leigh's condition would be thinking only about their race for survival, not about their next race out on the roads. After all, twice during his hospital stay his family had been summoned to his bedside when things looked especially grim. But Allen Leigh is not like most people. Despite sustaining a coma, cracked ribs, a punctured lung, and the prospect of many weeks of intensive care and rehab, the grandfather of eleven was not about to let an automobile accident keep him from one day returning to his life's passion. "I may have been naïve about it and I'm not sure the doctors thought so, but there was no doubt at all in my mind I would go through recovery and get back to running like before," he says. It is no wonder, then, that Allen's Leigh's best race was the first one he ran after that accident, although it took him two long years to get back to the starting line.

The beginning of Allen's running career coincided with the running boom of the 1970s. By then he was in his late thirties and began running on the recommendation of his doctor to relieve stiff joints. His gear of choice at the time? Army boots. After joining a running club at work, he was introduced to a few things that changed his life: comfortable running shoes and the teachings of Dr. George Sheehan. Allen was particularly inspired by an essay from the popular running philosopher about "listening to your body," in which Sheehan advocates "pace" instead of "speed," and expounds on the basic training questions of how fast, how far, and how often. "His comments were so much in alignment with my own thinking and made so much common sense that I decided to apply them to my life," says Allen, "which is why I never had any injuries attributable to running."

As a tribute to Sheehan, Allen began the website runninginjuryfree.com, where he dispenses his own unique brand of running wisdom. Even more followers flock to his companion blog, oldmanrunning.org, which is subtitled, "A look at my reentry into distance running that teaches the basics of running via the experiences of a seventy-seven-year-old geezer." It is that reentry into distance running—not after a running injury but after the automobile accident—that consumes the life of this one-time 7-minute-per-mile runner. A reentry that reached a milepost with his running of the Great Salt Lake Half Marathon on August 19, 2006.

Today Allen doesn't talk much about the accident that nearly killed him. He would rather talk about how the strength and stamina from thirty years of running saved his life, and how focused he became on picking up where he left off. "I literally had to start from scratch," he says, when recalling the effort to regain his running form. "From wheelchair, to crutches, to pulling myself up the stairs by the banister, to finally walking on my own. The first time I tried to do a run I could only do an eighth of a mile before getting tired." Slowly, as Allen's strength and aerobic capacity increased, that eighth of a mile run became a half mile and then a full mile. The Dr. George Sheehan disciple then began patiently following the "ten percent rule," which states that runners should never increase their weekly mileage by more than ten percent over the previous week's total. Allen also alternated "heavy" training days with "light" days or rest days, in order to give his mending body sufficient time to adjust to each new level of stress.

By the time he decided to finally enter a race, Allen had several long, slow runs and middle distance runs under his belt. He knew then that it was as good a time as any to attempt the 13.1-mile distance. What he didn't know until he registered for the half marathon was the significance of the race date itself: August 19th was two years to the day from Allen's struggle through that first eighth-of-a-mile run after his accident.

The Great Salt Lake Half Marathon offers participants the chance to run across the largest salt lake in the western hemisphere. The race begins at 6:30 a.m. and follows a USATF-certified, point-to-point course that includes a 7-mile paved causeway across the Great Salt Lake to the white sandy beaches of Antelope Island. The course is mostly flat, with a few short inclines in the last two miles. If the 13.1-mile distance isn't daunting enough for some runners, the thin air can also be a factor, as the course elevation hovers around 4,500 feet in altitude.

"Since the race started before daylight, I didn't know how fast I was going at first since it was too dark to read my GPS," says Allen. "After a couple of miles there was enough daylight to see what my pace was, and I couldn't believe it!" During his training runs leading up to the race, Allen was clocking about twelve and a half minutes per mile. Now, with the excitement of his first race in years and the usual race day adrenaline rush, he was churning out each mile at a pace three minutes faster—a pace he held for the next several miles. "After eight miles I was tired and had to slow down. Starting with mile nine, I began to take walking breaks every mile," a strategy now recommended for runners of all ages and abilities in races of any distance.

"The last mile made a big left turn going onto the island. In my training I always ran the last 100 yards faster—like a tempo run—and I put in a spurt at the end so I was able to come in at a pretty good pace. I was pleased to get first place in my age group, but since I was the only one that age, my son told me I was also *last* in my age group," he recalls with a chuckle. Nevertheless, Allen's time of 2:21:16 enabled him to achieve his goal of running under two hours and thirty minutes.

But perhaps his most important goal was realized two years earlier when he took the first stride of that first run of an eighth of a mile. What was it that helped him get to that point, and eventually to the finish line of a half marathon? "I always enjoyed running and had the discipline to stay with it," he says. "My mindset was that this was just a normal thing that I should be doing in my life." Some runners, after months or even years of physical and emotional investment in preparation for that special, life-affirming race, see everything beyond that achievement as anticlimactic. Not Allen. "I'm almost seventy-eight years old," he says, "and this race helped get me back on my routine. Now I've got at least twenty-two more years of running to do!"

Running Tip: "Run because you enjoy it. It makes no difference whether you stop running to watch the ducks in the river or you run as fast as you can to set a new personal best. Run for the pleasure and enjoy all of it."

Alvina Begay

2012 Payton Jordan Cardinal Invitational 10,000 Meters

"In our culture we have holy people who are up before the sun," says Navajo Alvina Begay. "So we were told that if we go running before the sunrise, they would see us and bless us and answer our prayers. When I was younger I really believed that if I got up every morning and ran I would get everything I wanted. It wasn't until I got older that I understood it better. Running before sunrise was really a way of teaching us about self-discipline, working hard towards a goal, and being comfortable with the uncomfortable. That's what they meant when they told us our prayers would be answered."

Running was the norm for Alvina on the reservation in Northeastern Arizona where she was born. "My dad was a good runner in the 1980s," she says, "and I grew up watching him run and train and go to races on weekends. My parents would always make us get up early and go running, and they had me run in the Navajo puberty ceremony when I was twelve. There the girls had to run three times a day—morning, afternoon, and night—for four straight days. So growing up it just seemed natural for me to run and compete." Running for Ganado High School, Alvina won state championships in cross-country and the 1,500 and 3,200 meters. She then attended Adams State and Arizona State Universities, where she excelled in both running and academics.

Alvina's plans for continuing her running career after college, or any career for that matter, were met with resistance by some in the Navajo community. "There are cultural expectations, especially for women," she says. "I even have family members asking when I'm going to settle down and have kids. At my age

I'm supposed to have three to five kids by now. But I'm lucky with the parents I have. My father encouraged me to focus on my running as long as I could, and both parents supported me and encouraged me and allowed me to keep doing what I was doing." And that included following her dreams.

"Billy Mills (a Native American and gold medalist in the 10,000 meters at the 1964 Olympics) is somebody who was a hero to me growing up," says Alvina, "and when I was a kid I had dreams of competing in the Olympic Trials at the University of Oregon's Hayward Field." Alvina's post-college successes, however, came mainly in the half marathon and marathon. In 2007 she finished 10th in the New York City Marathon and eventually qualified for both the 2008 and 2012 Olympic Trials at that distance. Of course, the marathon trials are run on the road and not at venerable Hayward Field. "Leading up to the London Olympics I got to work with Alberto Salazar (the elite coach and former world-class marathoner) to get ready for the marathon trials," she says. "He showed me how hard I can push myself, and I mean both physically and mentally. He would give me these workouts that I would be scared to death of. I thought, 'How am I going to survive this?' But I would do it, and when I was finished with that workout he'd throw something else in there." Although she learned a lot from the legendary runner and coach, Alvina was not able to finish in one of the coveted top three spots to qualify for the Olympic team. "When I didn't make the marathon team that January, I decided to have fun and enjoy running the rest of the year. I didn't have a lot of expectations for the year or time goals. When I went to the Cardinal Invitational at Stanford to run my first 10,000 meters on the track in years, my goal was just to run a personal best. I was more a half marathoner and a marathoner; I didn't consider myself a 10K runner." Because she hadn't run a 10,000-meter race in several years, and because her previous times at that distance were, in her words, "horrible," Alvina was placed in the "B" heat of the 10K with those expected to run slower than those in the "A" heat.

Out of curiosity, Alvina asked a friend how fast she would

have to run in order to be invited to the Olympic Trials at that distance. "I didn't even know what the Olympic Trials qualifying time was for the 10K," she admits. "My friend told me that to qualify for the trials I had to run 32:45. Then I asked her what the split times were and when she told me I thought, 'I can do that.' When I started the race I felt uncomfortable for the first couple of laps. I remember thinking, 'Oh goodness this is going to be a long race.' Then suddenly I just felt really good. With that race, if I felt that something was off for a lap or a mile, I was really good about telling myself to calm down and not let it get to me. I was able to put my frame of mind back to the positive. I didn't let the negative take over." Like she had learned on those early morning runs on the reservation before sunrise, Alvina was simply "being comfortable with the uncomfortable."

"We were in a big pack and I felt really good so I just broke the race down into miles and focused on running the race one mile at a time. Every time I looked at a split I was right at the time for the Olympic Trials qualifying standard, and I was getting excited. But a little past halfway in the race we slowed down. I was still with the group but the times were getting slower. I remember my coach told me not to lead, not to push the pace until two miles to go, so I had to make a really quick decision: to follow my coach's race plan or go after that qualifying time."

Alvina's decision was to follow her dream and not her coach's plan, and that meant in her "B" heat she would have to cover the remaining laps like an "A" runner. "I just took off," she recalls. "I took over the race and the lead and gapped everybody right away, and then I got back on pace. I thought the girls behind were going to come and get me or that I was going to hit a wall, but I felt really good and really light. As I focused on one mile at a time I noticed I was getting faster, and every time I saw that I was on pace with my split times it just made me want to run even faster. I remember hearing the announcer say with less than a mile to go that I was well under the qualifying standard, and I just kept thinking to myself, 'Don't screw this up! Just hold on and finish the race.' With one lap to go I just threw down a kick and won the heat."

What mattered most, however, was not her finishing place but her finishing time. When she looked at the clock she realized she had not only run a personal best, but had come in eleven seconds faster than the qualifying standard; Alvina was finally going to run at Hayward Field. "I was shocked and very, very happy," she recalls. "I just felt really excited and happy after all those years of hard work and the time I spent working with Alberto Salazar. He was a tough coach but I felt that everything he made me do paid off. The reason why it was such a spectacular race for me was that I really didn't have any goals except running for a personal best. When I don't have the pressure and I'm just having fun with it, those are the times I race the best. I just had a relaxed vibe going into that meet."

Will Navajo children now look up to her the way she looked up to Billy Mills in her youth? "I hope so," she says, "we need kids to be inspired." To that end, Alvina has taken on the role as an ambassador for Nike N7, a program that is committed to introducing the benefits of sports to Native American and Aboriginal communities in the United States and Canada. "In addition to being a pro runner, I have a degree in nutrition and I'm a registered dietician," she says. "I give a lot of talks on nutrition and encourage Native Americans to be active and healthy, especially the youth and the children."

On June 22, 2012 in Eugene, Oregon, Alvina failed to finish among the top three runners in the 10,000-meter run and therefore did not make the Olympic team. Nevertheless, she had achieved her goal of racing at Hayward Field in the Olympic Trials, a feat that would be the highlight of most runners' careers. "It was a dream come true," she says. "The last couple of years I didn't think it was going to happen. I don't have a lot of speed to run that quick on the track, and after not believing or having faith that I could ever make it to the track trials, it was such a big deal to finally do it. My race at the Invitational where everything seemed to go perfectly comes along once in a great while. It was one of those races you pray for." And whether or not you believe holy people can see you running, we know somehow that prayer was answered.

Running Tip: "Have fun with running. Many people start running because it's fun and there are no expectations. I think if you can get yourself back to that time, everything will fall into place and you can have a great running experience. At my level, when racing and training becomes a career, you can easily forget that. You have to remind yourself that you're doing it for fun."

Gerry Lindgren

Gerry Lindgren was hearing footsteps. No matter how fast the skinny American kid circled the cinder track, he couldn't seem to shake the powerful Soviets who were stalking him. Of course, nobody expected the eighteen-year-old to be leading the veteran Soviet runners so late in the race. "Everyone knew those guys were the best in the world," recalls Gerry, "and I had never even run the 10,000 meters before." But Gerry was running with a chip on his shoulder. "The Russians called us lazy Americans because we could win the sprints but could never beat them in the longer races, so I decided to take the lead and try to dispel that image. I wasn't going to slow down." Still, even after running one lap faster than the last, and the next one even faster, he couldn't escape the noisy footsteps of the Russians right behind him.

Just a few years earlier Gerry had been considered the slowest member of his cross-country team at Spokane's John Rogers High School. "My coach said I was the skinniest, wimpiest, most unlikely athlete he had ever seen," recalls Gerry. "I wanted to quit, but the coach found a way that I could help the team." On long training runs Gerry would play the rabbit. He would start ahead of the others who would then have to chase him down to avoid the embarrassment of losing to the scrawny sophomore. The strategy, however, had an unintended result. "I took the challenge and found out that no one could ever catch me," says Gerry, "and in no time I was the best kid on our team. I always hated myself for being such a wimpy kid, and I wanted to find something in my life that I could actually do well. At that point I got the idea that it could be running."

Although he wasn't adding many pounds to his slight frame, Gerry started adding victories and state records to his running resume, in distances from the mile to the 5,000 meters. Joining an Amateur Athletic Union team after high school, he began following a running regimen of three-a-day workouts: a long run in the morning, quarter-mile repeats on the track before lunch, then another long run at night. The weekly mileage totals were unheard of at that time, especially for a young runner, but Gerry seemed to thrive on the intense training. And when his coach needed another long distance runner for the USA vs. USSR Dual Track Meet of 1964, Gerry was chosen for the 10K.

"I was scared to death," he says, when he recalls standing in front of 40,000 spectators at the LA Coliseum before the start of the race. "I had no idea how to run the 10,000 meters, so my coach told me to just try and stay with the two Russians for at least four miles. But as soon as the gun sounded all the nervousness I felt at the start just went away. I knew then I had a job to do. The Russians immediately took off for the lead and I fell in behind them in third place."

Leonid Ivanov and Anatoly Dutov continued to run together at the front for two-thirds of the race. "They kept looking back at me and talking to one another," recalls Gerry, "and I just stayed where I was." Just before four miles one of them took off creating a gap between first and second place. "I started wondering if I should go around and catch up with the first one or stay where I was. Then someone on the sideline yelled, 'Coach says if you're feeling good go on by,' so I took off around the Russian in second place and went after the first one. When I caught him, I just ran right by him. When both my feet were in the air I could hear the grinding of the cinders on the track, so I knew those were his steps and that he had come up right behind me. I kept going as fast as I could go for another lap but I could still hear him back there." Gary wasn't sure whether one or both Soviet runners were behind him, nor how far back they were, because he didn't want to look. "I ran another sprint lap and stumbled a couple of times, but I didn't want them to see me look back and think I was weakening. When I passed my coach on the sidelines I held my arms apart and pointed behind me, for him to indicate how much of a lead I had."

What Gerry thought he heard was "120 yards," but he knew that couldn't be right. "I knew that was wrong because I could still hear them on the cinders behind me. When I began the final lap I couldn't believe I was still in the lead, and when I came to the final straightaway I just sprinted as hard as I could to the finish." In doing so, Gerry became the first American to win the 10,000 meters since the USA vs. USSR series began. When Gerry finally turned to look around, it was what he *didn't* see that surprised him. "I looked back and there were no Russians." Indeed, Ivanov, running for second place, was still about 100 yards behind. But there was another surprise. "I began to cool down with a jog and noticed that every time I took a step I didn't hear the crunch of the cinders until after my foot was in the air again. I realized then that for those last three miles of the race, no one was behind me—it was my own feet I was hearing!"

When the result of his race against the Soviets made headlines across the nation, it stirred the imaginations of thousands of young runners, which is why Gerry still considers it the best race he ever ran. "That race has stayed with me because of the effect it had on other runners in the mid '60s. I think my winning inspired them to train harder and to realize that if someone like me can compete with the best in the world, they can too." Forty years later, due in part to the tenacious running style he exhibited in that race and throughout his stellar career, Gerry Lindgren was inducted into the USA Track and Field Hall of Fame. Not bad for a wimpy kid.

Running Tip: "You have to build a strong base. The more miles you get in the stronger you become. No matter how much speed work you do, you'll be in trouble at the end of the race if you don't have a good base."

Jon Sinclair

Seinfeld fans can easily recall the popular episode in which George Costanza changed his life for the better by doing the *opposite* of what he normally would do. The theory was that if every instinct George had was wrong, then the opposite would have to be right. But before there was *Seinfeld* there was Sinclair. Jon Sinclair. In the most important race of his young career, Jon did the opposite, and it changed his life forever.

Jon gravitated to organized running for the same reason countless others became runners; he was not good enough or big enough for any other sport. "I had no hand-eye coordination," he says. "I was terrible at baseball, too short for basketball, and too small for football, but I always liked running." After he was coaxed onto the track team because a third runner was needed to compete in the mile, he promptly won his first race in near record time. With coaching and experience, Jon continued his winning ways and eventually became one of the top runners in the state of Colorado at Arvada West High School. Leading up to the state championships his junior year, however, Jon still didn't know just how good he could be. "I was winning most of my races, but there were a lot of guys in the state I had not yet run against. Most people when they looked at me didn't see a champion runner, and that was my own self image too. Against the best in the state, I certainly would not be a favorite."

After doing well in a qualifying heat to advance to the state finals, Jon gained some confidence in his abilities compared to those other milers. "I remember thinking to myself after the prelims that I could win it," he says. "When I told that to my dad and some friends it was met with skeptical silence, but in my head I thought I could win." Anyone with thoughts of winning the state championship in the mile, however, would have to get past Bob Fink, a senior and the prohibitive favorite. "Nobody had beaten him all year," recalls Jon, "and he had the fastest times of anyone. But he ran the same race every time and his strategy never changed. He'd go out like a bat out of hell, really hard. His second lap would be a little bit slower for him to recover. The third lap he practically "walked" to prepare for the final lap, and that last lap he'd just kick really hard at the end. He ran that way every single time, and every single time he'd win. The others would go out really hard with him, then everyone would calm down and the pack would bunch up for the next two laps, and in the fourth lap he would just outkick everyone. So I devised a strategy that I thought would work, although it was pretty unorthodox. I decided that I was going to do just the opposite.

"At the starting line I remember being nervous and anxious, but I don't know if that was any different from any other race. There wasn't any expectation that I would win. If I finished third or fourth people would have thought that was probably about right. Even though I had only lost one race all season, there were a whole lot of runners in that race who had faster times than me. No one would have looked at me as being the guy to beat, so I didn't have that kind of pressure on me."

According to plan, Jon stayed at the back of the pack for the first quarter mile instead of going out fast with the favorite. When Bob, the leader, slowed in the second lap to recover, Jon used that interval to catch up. "I was on his shoulder coming down the stretch," recalls Jon, "and at the end of the half mile, the beginning of the third lap, I just took off and ran as hard as I could. I was sprinting, and I immediately gapped the field because everybody was watching what Bob was doing. And Bob did the same thing as he always did on that lap, he slowed down. I got ahead by five yards, then ten yards and fifteen yards, and when we came down the stretch I was way out in the lead." On the final lap, Jon had to continue his all-out, pedal-to-the-metal dash he had begun a lap earlier in order to counter the powerful kick he knew was coming from the favorite.

"I can look back on that race and remember it so well," says Jon. "On the back stretch I kept thinking to myself, 'returning champion, returning champion,' like a mantra. But at the end of the backstretch I was tying up a little but still sprinting as hard as I could; I knew Bob was going to be coming up that home stretch and coming really hard. I could hear the crowd screaming. Bob probably started his sprint with four hundred yards to go and was now probably beginning to panic because he was going to have a hard time catching me unless I really died. I had been running flat out from the half mile on, and at the end coming upon the final stretch I was completely toast, but I was going to go all out until Bob went by me. I didn't understand physiology then. I really didn't understand what my strengths and weaknesses were. But I had devised the best strategy I possibly could based on my own abilities and given who I was running against. If the race had been another fifteen yards we would have been shoulder to shoulder at the end, but he just couldn't make up the gap. I beat him at the finish by about five feet." Jon's winning time was 4:21.8.

"I always come back to that day because all the other performances in my career, professionally and collegiately, hinge on that race," he says. "It was the beginning of much bigger things because I proved to myself that I was capable of winning big races and that I was a quality runner. And I guess it taught me a lesson. It taught me that winning is often not being the best guy, but being the smartest guy. Throughout my career I've beaten people just by being smarter. Knowing when to go, and doing unorthodox things. More than anything, that race taught me to measure myself against other people and what those other people can do, and then figure out ways to beat them based on that."

Indeed, if anyone knows how to beat people, it's Jon Sinclair. In his career as a professional, he recorded more wins than any other male runner in modern road racing history. He is also a former USA National Cross-Country and 10,000-meter champion, and is a member of the Road Runners Club of America Hall of Fame.

"Most runners run against themselves to get a personal best," he says, "not against anyone else. But as a pro runner it was always how much money could I make beating people, so I had to run head-to-head. That state championship was really the first time I did that. It showed me how important that was and also that I could win like that. It changed my whole life, it really did."

Running Tip: "You have to expect that your first or second or third race is not going to be as good as subsequent races. It's a learning process; you need more than one race to get used to the environment, the starting line, different ways of warming up, what you can eat before the race, and all you have to do to get to the starting line and feel comfortable. If a client comes to me and says they want to be ready for a big race somewhere in the future, they really need four or five races leading up to it to really be ready."

Lisa Rainsberger

Professional runners make it look easy. Out front in the lead pack with their eyes focused straight ahead, their faces betray no hint of discomfort as they effortlessly churn out mile after mile before sprinting comfortably to the finish line, barely out of breath. Or so it seems. But if Lisa Rainsberger's Chicago Marathon is any indication, professional runners go through the same range of emotions (grief, joy), insecurities ("Did I make a mistake?") and wayward thoughts (Richard Simmons?) as the rest of us; they just do it at a faster pace.

The last American woman to win the Boston Marathon thought the cards were stacked against her right from the start of the 1989 Chicago Marathon. "I went into the race having been the champion the previous year," says Lisa. "There's that burden you bear of the expectations from the organizers and yourself and your coaches when you've won it before. It was also a very competitive field, including an American who had beaten me handily in some races that year." Not only that, the temperature was already a balmy 68 degrees when she awoke that October day. And something else she discovered that morning was equally disconcerting. "I woke up that morning to a surprise. As a woman you always have to think about this and the timing of things, and for me it was the wrong time of month." Since her sponsor, New Balance, had all-white uniforms that year, it just added to her uneasiness. "The odds were really against me that day."

Lisa could sense it was going to be a fast pace as soon as the gun went off. "There was no holding back," she says. "It was quick the year before, but this year the women were close to a

2:23 marathon pace right from the start. I'd like to think that I could run that pace but I knew that wasn't going to happen. So I had to make a decision to fall back and run the pace I had trained for. I had that intrinsic feeling of being able to sustain it." Lisa was already thirty seconds behind the six women in the lead group by the time she saw her coach and her husband at the five-mile mark. "They were standing there and I could just read their body language that they were really concerned for me. But I had to trust my instincts and let those girls go."

Lisa could trust her instincts due to the success of her training regimen leading up to the race, a regimen based on a unique philosophy. "A lot of people get their confidence from the number of miles they run," she says. "I got my confidence from the number of *minutes I run under race pace*. I didn't want to be really good at running slow. I wanted to be really good at running fast. Even if I did a ten-second sprint, I would count that. So for me, it was a calculation of how many minutes I ran under marathon pace vs. how many overall miles I ran; quality vs. quantity. And that way I could feel the tipping point; if I'm doing too many miles, I'm not getting the quality that I need. That's my secret, so don't tell."

Five miles later, the thirty-second gap had increased to fifty seconds, and Lisa let her concentration wander. At the time it was probably not a good idea. "I could see the TV helicopter way in the distance following the leaders," she says. "It was really disheartening to see it when I was so far back. But I kept looking at my watch telling myself that I wasn't doing anything wrong. It was a hot day and I was still on my personal best pace, so I just had to tune out all that clutter and focus. What I boiled it down to was one person at a time. I thought to myself that I just needed to get on the podium, win place or show, because then I would be respectable and I could live with myself."

Lisa's patience began to pay off as some of the runners who went out too fast in the unseasonably hot weather began to fade. "Soon enough, one by one I would catch somebody. I realized I did the right thing by not going out with them because they were all coming back. One woman I caught and passed was wearing all black. I thought, 'How stupid is that?' I was wearing white and by then I was *glad* I was wearing white! All those mental thoughts worked through my head. I was going to beat her because I was smarter; I was wearing white. By mile fifteen I was in third place and a mile later I passed another woman, still running my same pace, very methodical and very calculating." And no longer was the TV helicopter hopelessly far away in the distance. "By mile eighteen the helicopter was right over me!

"At that point in the Chicago Marathon we were in an ethnic neighborhood with so many smells and sounds, and there were a lot of turns," says Lisa. "I remember coming around the corner and realized, damn, there she is, the leader. It was Cathy O'Brien who had beaten me all season and had set a world record at ten miles. So I was energized. I came up and got my water bottle, saw my family, and after I had a drink I just took off into the lead." Once in the lead at mile eighteen, Lisa felt invincible and believed no one would catch her. But then she came to mile twenty-three. "At mile twenty-three it became so hot," she recalls. Back then they had started using Gatorade on race courses, but the aid stops were at every 5K, so the fluids were few and far between. I was in a back part of the course and there were not many spectators, but it was sunny and there was no shade and there were no fluids. I went from that whole confident, swaggering attitude to, 'Oh no! Did I make a mistake?' I was afraid the fat lady was beginning to sing for me. I didn't know how far my lead was, but I didn't want to think I had a sizeable lead because that's the moment when you surrender. I just continued to run as if she were right behind me."

Lisa never did look back because she was looking ahead trying to find that next water stop, or for anything that would take her mind off of her predicament. "In the last three miles I remember there was a guy who had this red-and-white striped jersey on," she says, "the kind that Richard Simmons would wear. I really didn't want to be seen with him in pictures at the finish line—that's what I was thinking! So I kept pressing and pressing and finally caught and passed him. Then at twenty-five miles I told myself, 'I can run fast for a mile.' Up until that point

I was so far away from the finish line I didn't feel I could run fast enough to reach it in first place. But with a mile to go, I told myself, 'It's just four times around the track.' It was all those things that I thought to myself during the race that helped me get to the finish.

"When I crossed the line I was so happy. There were all those insecurities I had been feeling before the race had even started, but at the finish I was able to really just share that moment. And I remember the race announcer was going crazy that an American had won, and someone with the American flag ran beside me across the finish line, so my race was topped off with that patriotism and that feeling of pride." Lisa's winning time of 2:28 was two minutes faster than her closest competitor.

"Sometimes the race is easy and you win and you accomplish exactly what you set out to do. This race really stands out for me because all the odds were against me. It's my best race in the sense that it captured all my emotions. I had to really dig deep down in mind and body and spirit to get where I wanted to be. At the end when I put it all together that's when it became the critical race for me. Now I use that race as a benchmark for my own coaching. The whole emotional spectrum that I went through for those two hours and twenty-eight minutes is something I can recall and use to teach about perseverance and trusting our instincts and knowing our abilities based on our training."

One question remains: Did Lisa finally get that drink her body craved in those final critical miles? "I did, and at the award ceremony I even made the comment that if it hadn't been for Gatorade I don't know how I would have finished. Two days after I returned home a huge truck showed up at my house and delivered all these boxes and cartons of free Gatorade. I joked that the next time I would say, 'If it hadn't been for that Mercedes…'"

Running Tip: "You can't be a workout chaser. You can't log on to the Internet and read about what everyone else is doing. You just have to tune all that out and focus on what's right for you. Some of the professionals I used to coach would come to me and say, 'I read so and so was doing this and I think I need to be doing this.' They were losing track of their own program and constantly chasing someone else's program, so they lost confidence in what they were doing. Develop a program with your coach and stick to it."

Jason Karp

He is the author of *Running a Marathon for Dummies*, but no one felt more like a dummy than Jason Karp when he was left in the dust by members of a rival cross-country team back in high school. Yet Jason claims it was his best race for what it taught him, and over the years, the nationally recognized running coach and personal trainer has used what he learned that day to help him and others be better runners.

In his youth, Jason Karp was not only interested in running but in learning how and why someone can put one foot in front of the other faster than someone else. "Ever since I started running track as a kid I became interested in the science behind athletic performance," he says. "What makes one person run faster than another, jump farther, and how does a baseball pitcher throw a curve? So when I graduated high school I wanted to go where I could study the science of sports." Jason eventually earned a Ph.D. in exercise physiology, began coaching, and authored five books. A few of those books, including *101 Winning Racing Strategies for Runners*, and some of his coaching principles, were no doubt influenced in part by what happened back in high school on that cross-country course.

"We didn't have a very good cross-country team," recalls Jason, "but I was by far the best runner we had, and I started winning a lot of races that season as a junior." Since Jason's team was part of a small private-school league that did not compete with the numerous public school teams in the area, Jason's exploits were soon on the radar of rival coaches. "I guess I was a little naïve because I didn't think other coaches knew about me or were planning on ways to beat me," he says. Jason learned that lesson the hard way in a dual meet that fall against Steinert High School.

According to Jason, "The coach at this school we were racing against knew who I was and had his team basically stalk me during the race. It was afterward when I learned what their plan was. I took the lead as soon as the race started but there were about five or six runners from the other school running in a pack right with me. Nobody else from my school was there." Never finding the need to come up with a race strategy in his previous victories, Jason stayed in the lead throughout most of the 5K race, unaware that the opposing team was strategizing against *him*.

"With a half mile to go they made this decisive move and went right by me, and I couldn't respond because it took me by surprise," he says. "There I was leading the pack as usual and thinking everything was going well and then they all went right by me. I was all by myself and they all ended up finishing ahead of me. They sat and kicked and I wasn't ready for it, and I felt like a fool that I was taken advantage of like that. But I also thought that it was pretty clever on the part of their coach to have a plan going into the race. I talked to those guys after the race and they revealed what had happened. They said their coach had told them what to do.

"So after that, I became more aware of what's going on in a race, more aware of when people make moves, and learned not to take things for granted. The race stands out because it was a real learning experience about the strategy that's involved in a race, rather than just going out and running fast. I didn't think a lot about that stuff back then." In his coaching, and in his racing, Jason has never stopped using the lessons he learned that day. "If I'm running with someone, I strategize and try to make a move that's unexpected. Or I'll use someone else to help me hold the pace in the middle of the race then pick a place to make a decisive move so that they don't have time to respond. So I find myself doing the same thing that was done to me all those year ago."

Switching gears, it would be remiss *not* to solicit some free training advice from this exercise physiologist, running coach, and running author. When asked what he considered the number one thing distance runners do wrong when it comes to their training, this was Jason's reply: "Competitive runners do their 'easy' runs too quickly. They don't train with polarity. By that I mean the 'easy' days should be very easy and the 'hard' days should be very hard, but a lot of runners feel guilty that they run too slow on their easy days. They don't realize that it's the recovery that allows them to adapt to the training and get faster, so they think they always have to push the pace. All the adaptations happen when you're *not* running, rather than when you are running."

Jason suggests that much of the problem comes from not understanding what the purpose of the workout is. "Most runners really don't understand why they are doing the workout a certain way," he adds. "They don't know the physiology and biochemistry behind the training so they don't understand why doing a workout a certain way will get a certain result. The easy days must be easy for a variety of reasons, the least of which is that it allows you to get more out of your harder days."

Running Tip: "Understand what the purpose of each day and each workout is. A lot of runners are far away from their potential and far away from what they can accomplish, but they tend to think they know it all. Understand what it is you're trying to accomplish and train smart. Train at optimum levels of effort rather than trying to run yourself into the ground every day."

Pam Reed

2002 Badwater Ultramarathon

1. Go slow
2. Drink plenty of club soda
3. Keep eating
4. Don't stop running for 135 miles

That was Pam Reed's recipe for surviving her first attempt at the longest, hottest, baddest endurance race anywhere on the planet. How well did it work? The forty-one-year-old wife and mother not only survived the race, she finished first. And not just first among females, but first *overall* … by nearly five hours!

In all her years as a competitive runner, Pam Reed had never even heard of a race called the Badwater Ultramarathon. "Chuck, a friend of mine, had been a race marshal at Badwater and said I should try it sometime," recalls Pam. "I said, 'What's Badwater?' So he told me and I said, 'NO WAY!'" What Chuck told her was that the race starts at the lowest and driest elevation in the Western Hemisphere, where temperatures can reach a lung-searing 130 degrees Fahrenheit, and finishes 135 miles later halfway up Mt. Whitney, the highest mountain peak in the Lower Forty-eight. The course follows three mountain ranges for a total of 13,000 feet of cumulative vertical ascent and 4,700 feet of cumulative descent. Along the way it visits places named Furnace Creek and Devil's Cornfield, where rubber soles can melt, gel oozes out of shoes, and sweat dries before it can cool the skin.

"I went home and told my husband about it," she says. "Then we watched a documentary about the race called *Running on the Sun*. The filmmaker's portrayal of the race made it look so dramatic, but I knew it couldn't be that bad. I was living in Tucson and training all the time in the dryness and the heat. I'd run in the morning, the afternoon, and the evening, and when I say 'heat' I mean 105 degrees Fahrenheit. It's when my body is at its best." Consequently, Pam came around to view the race as just one more challenge in her ultramarathon career, a career that already included numerous 100-mile races and an Ironman Triathlon. "So I called Chuck and told him I'd do it."

Chuck began putting together a support crew that would follow Pam and supply all the essentials she would need for a race that could last two and a half days. Pam would supply whatever knowledge she had accumulated from her previous races. "Before I came to Badwater I had done over twenty 100-mile races," she says, "so I had a lot of experience for what I could and couldn't do." One thing she could do was go slow, something she learned before ever attempting her first 100-mile race. "My husband once had a client who was sixty years old and was running 100-mile races. I thought that was crazy. But then I went running with him and he showed me how he did it. I learned from him to go slow, that it's not marathon pace; that's the key. And I've learned that I'm not that fast anyway, so I have to keep going. I don't stop and I never sit down."

From all those long races, Pam also learned what did and didn't work in terms of refueling her body on the run. "For me, the more I eat the better," she says. "A nutritionist friend told me that runners have to keep food in their gut because if they stop eating, the stomach shuts down and doesn't want to take anything. I eat little bits continually. Some honey, bread, Ensure, and tomato soup. Another thing I learned from a doctor was to keep my stomach moving, meaning burping and passing gas. When your stomach stops moving, that's when people throw up. I found drinking club soda rather than water really helps me with that, and it has sodium too."

And what about caring for her feet? Extrapolating from findings of the American Academy of Podiatric Sports Medicine, Pam's feet would hit the ground about 200,000 times during her 135-mile run at Badwater, with a force of three to four times her body weight. But Pam had a strict no-nonsense policy when it came to her heels and toes. "I made a decision long ago that I wasn't going to play around with my feet. I'm not touching them. When you screw around with your feet they just start hurting again, so what good does it do? And I never change my shoes during a race; I just keep going."

Keeping her going through the desert and over the mountains was the job of the support crew that would follow her along the course in a van. As David Letterman joked when Pam was a guest on his show, "You can't have aid stations along the route because people waiting for the competitors in the sun and the heat would die." As Pam recalls, "I kind of felt embarrassed by all the help I got. In a sense, Badwater was easier than other ultra races because in those you have to carry stuff with you and you never see anybody for long stretches. At Badwater, the crew was with me the whole time." Still, leading up to the race, Pam knew that having a good crew and being physically ready were just two components needed for such a grueling endeavor. "I knew you can't take it for granted," she says. "You've got to be smart because a lot of factors come into play, and at this point in my life, mental preparation is ninety percent."

Pam went off with the 6:00 a.m. starting group, while other competitors followed at 8:00 a.m. and 10:00 a.m. "Chuck decided every quarter mile his crew would spray me with cold water and give me food," she says. "They really took care of me." Pam reached the first checkpoint at Furnace Creek having passed several of those who started with her. Then after the first major climb, she was in first place among her group without even realizing it. "After mile forty and the town of Stovepipe Wells there is a twenty-mile climb," she recalls. "What happens in Badwater is that on the hills some people walk up, but I do this little jog. I love hills. I just kept passing people. Then there was nobody around. We kept thinking that there's somebody ahead of us, there had to be." Despite no other runners being around her, Pam was not lonely; her expert crew was always nearby to give her companionship and attend to her needs. "My crew and I had so much fun," she says, "and Chuck was real anal about being prepared. The reason runners are getting such good finishing times today is because Chuck and his crew showed everybody how to do it. They set the standard. The other teams were doing it all wrong." Pam had been on the course for about fourteen hours as day turned into night, but was in good enough spirits to enjoy the scenery. "On the first climb in the dark it's beautiful," she recalls. "It's so funny how people perceive Death Valley. The landscape is gorgeous, but some people just think it's ugly. And the stars at night, it's really cool." Little did Pam know that she was on her way to becoming a star herself.

At a certain point, based on the pace and course location of the runners in the two remaining starting groups, Pam became the virtual leader of the race in terms of overall time. "At the third checkpoint, which is Panamint Springs, there is another twenty-mile climb but I had absolutely no problem with it," she says. "Then at mile 100, the race director came up on his motorcycle and said that if I kept it up, I was going to win the whole thing. We didn't know that we were winning because so many had started two and four hours behind me. I asked how I can be winning when there were runners who started four hours after me, and he said there was no way they could catch me in overall time. So I just started to speed up because it was so exciting and it was cool and it was just getting light out."

Though no other runners in the race were anywhere near her, Pam found the road up the final climb congested. "The race director had called the *Los Angeles Times* and *The New York Times*, and on the final climb they started interviewing me and their photographers wanted pictures. My crew complained that they should at least let me finish the race." After 28 hours, 56 minutes, and 47 seconds—all without sleep—she crossed the finish line.

"At the finish I had this overwhelming sense of peace," she recalls. "It was really weird. Forever in my running I have always felt unsettled, that I could do more and do better, and finally I didn't have that feeling anymore. That race totally changed my life. I became more humble, and all of a sudden people started noticing me. It was such a cool and fun experience. But I noticed that when people recognized me they treated me nicer. I really try hard not to treat people any differently, whoever they are. That whole experience taught me to embrace people for what they do. We're all equal, and anyone on any given day can win. I feel so blessed that I can do this. You get humble, you don't get cocky."

Sometimes in a race, even one as demanding as Badwater, everything goes right. "It went perfectly well. It was like a fairytale. I told myself I'm never doing this again because it went too perfect and here I am again going into my tenth race!" Not surprisingly, Pam has had a few "imperfect" races at Badwater since that first one. There was the year she broke her sacrum, and the year she became so dehydrated in windy conditions that she lost ten pounds in forty miles and had to drop out. But if anyone wondered if her win at Badwater was a fluke, the answer came a year later when Pam finished first overall once again!

Running Tip: "Break up your long training runs. I see too many people getting injured. Instead of going on a twenty-mile run, go on two ten-mile runs: one in the morning and one in the afternoon. Or three seven-mile runs. I think that is part of the reason I have the longevity I have. The long runs take a lot out of you and you should save that for the race."

Cecily Tynan

The American Cancer Society estimates that in 2014, nearly 30,000 men will die of prostate cancer, and about 233,000 men will be newly diagnosed. After he was diagnosed in 2004, Sports Director Gary Papa of Philadelphia's ABC Affiliate, WPVI-TV, announced on-air that he was undergoing chemotherapy for the disease. Gary soon joined the board of Prostate Health International in the city to help generate prostate cancer awareness and educate the public about early detection and treatment. He was also instrumental in helping establish and promote the organization's Father's Day Run and fund-raiser for prostate cancer, before losing his six-year battle with the disease in 2009.

According to Cecily Tynan, an elite runner and the meteorologist at the station, Gary was more than just a colleague. "We both worked the six o'clock and eleven o'clock newscasts and did a public affairs show together," she says. "He wasn't just a coworker but a close friend too. We got to be like family." Eventually the 5K race was renamed the Gary Papa Run for Prostate Cancer, and it was the 2012 version of that event that Cecily Tynan calls her best race. "It wasn't a personal best or anything," she says, "but emotionally it was huge for me because I was always so close to Gary and I felt he was there with me."

Cecily never planned on being a runner. From the age of three through her mid-teens, Cecily's feet were adorned with ballet slippers rather than running shoes. It wasn't until her parents kept her home from her ballet company's tour of Russia that she joined the high school track team to keep herself occupied. "They put me on hurdles right away," she recalls, "because they figured if I was a ballet dancer I could leap. I absolutely loved it and progressed from there to some road races that summer." After high school she attended Washington and Lee University, where she ran the mile, the 4 x 400 relay, and cross-country. "It was a Division III school where academics were always important," she says, "so there really wasn't any pressure to run fast, which I think is great. For me, running has always been something I do for fun, and it remains fun. It has never really been like a job. I had some friends who ran for Division I schools, and they had to take cortisone injections and were anorexic and it really derailed their running careers. I'm still running now because I didn't destroy my body."

Cecily began running marathons with the cross-country team and later while working as the Meteorologist at WDBJ in Roanoke, Virginia. After a stint at KTMV in Las Vegas, she arrived in Philadelphia and joined a local women's running group where she took her running to the next level. "I began enjoying interval training and more intense workouts," she says. "I got to where I was pretty consistent in breaking three hours for the marathon and I started to think maybe I could make the Olympic Trials, but I just couldn't get past the two hour, fifty-four minute barrier." Now a Masters (over forty) runner, Cecily does most of her training—speed workouts, tempo runs, and seventy-five-minute long runs—during the week, since weekends are for her children. "My mileage is relatively low," she says, "but on the flip side it has kept me from having to battle a lot of injuries, and I'm actually a better runner now than I was in my twenties." Did studying ballet all those years help with her running? "I think it made me more aware of my body," she says. "It gave me discipline, which you need to be a good runner. Unfortunately it gave me really bad feet. My husband says I'm beautiful just from my head to my ankles."

Thoughts turned from her running to Gary Papa's running in the race that would eventually bear his name. "Gary ran a few years after his diagnosis, then when he got sick he walked it, and the last year he was only able to cheer people." But it is a testament to the outpouring of love and support for Gary and his charity that the race has grown from four hundred runners to over 4,000. The 5K out-and-back course begins near the Philadelphia Museum of Art, known among art aficionados as one of the best museums in the world, and among others as the home of the "Rocky" steps. It then parallels the Schuylkill River along part of the Philadelphia Marathon course before the turnaround.

According to Cecily, "All my best races are races where I hold back a little bit at the beginning. If I go out too fast the race is pretty much over. For this race I remember running pretty much consistent splits. I was just under six minutes for the first mile and I had all these people surging past me, then I began reeling them in. The strategy has worked in other races too. I finished third in the Disney World Marathon by just sticking with my plan and letting the other women go ahead of me, staying on a steady pace, and then reeling them in. So in this race I was picking off women and with maybe two hundred meters to go I passed a fellow Masters runner and won.

"It wasn't one of my fastest 5Ks, but it was a great race for me because I felt really proud and I felt Gary was cheering me on." Cecily was not only the top female (and 30th overall), but more importantly, the top fund-raiser in the race. "I'm amazed at the generosity of people. I have 35,000 Facebook fans and I say if everyone donates a dollar, look how much can be raised." In the 2014 race, more than $280,000 in donations and pledges was raised for Prostate Health International.

"The year Gary died, it was just three days before the race," she recalls. "I remember the morning of the race thinking I was going to have a really good result because if I start to hurt, I'm just going to think about what Gary went through fighting prostate cancer and that would make me go faster. But when I started to hurt that year I realized it was just a race, so it didn't matter; it was just not that important. But this race was several years after Gary had died and it was different. I think it made me feel closer to him. That maybe by winning it I felt his presence there. I just remember knowing that Gary was watching me, and it brought back some really good memories of him and our friendship."

Running Tip: "Just hold back a little bit in the beginning of the race. You have adrenaline, so the tendency is to run your first mile faster than the pace you planned to run. It's hard sometimes mentally when you see all these people running past you, but if you could just hold back a little bit you can pour it on in the middle and at the end of the race. Don't worry about what everyone else is doing. Just run a steady pace and you'll catch them."

Go to www.cancer.gov for the online booklet "What You Need to Know About Prostate Cancer" to learn about testing, treatment, and questions to ask your doctor.

Dan O'Connor

"I can't do this" were four words Dan O'Connor did not like hearing at the starting line of the 2010 Marine Corps Marathon. The words came from Zach Dunn, a wounded marine who was attempting his first race in a hand crank wheelchair. "He was very reluctant once we got to the starting line," says Dan. "I knew exactly what he was going through, so I calmed him down and said, 'Zach, even if it takes us all day, we're going to do this.'"

Dan knew what Zach was going through because he too was a wounded marine who had taken up wheelchair racing. Dan received severe leg wounds in Vietnam from an IED while leading a patrol. "I used to run track and cross-country in high school, but that ended real quick after 'Nam," he says. It didn't get any easier for Dan; several years after returning home he lost a leg in a motorcycle accident. Zach, a veteran of the Iraq War, suffered gun shot wounds, shrapnel wounds, and traumatic brain injury while serving in Falujah. "I got a call asking if I could ride along with Zach in the race because he has a lot of injuries and needed someone to do it with him," recalls Dan. "He didn't have the confidence to do it on his own."

By then Dan was a veteran of over twenty marathons in hand crank wheelchairs, and was coaching other wounded marines in the discipline as a way for them to stay active. And speaking of being active, Dan will tell you he's in better shape now in his late sixties than he was at thirty-five. Much of that is due to his relationship with Achilles International, the nonprofit where able-bodied volunteers and people with disabilities come together to train and race. It was at a convention for amputees where Dan was introduced to the Achilles program and the

161

hand crank wheelchair. "Achilles saved my life," he says. I wasn't physically active, I was overweight, I had lost my leg, and I had a bad attitude. Through Achilles I've done more on one leg than I ever did on two."

At the start, it wasn't just the physical challenge of going 26.2 miles by hand crank that bothered Zach. His reluctance had just as much to do with being around so many people. "A lot of veterans, especially from Iraq, are not comfortable in crowds," says Dan. "They are taught to avoid congested places where they are susceptible to IEDs and suicide bombers. I encouraged him to go to the runner's expo the day before, and he stayed very close to me the whole time." While the Marine Corps Marathon is known for a few nasty hills, it is also known for having one of the largest fields of any race, typically over 30,000 participants. For that reason wheelchair athletes are allowed to start well before the runners.

"We got started but he wasn't doing good at all; it was like he didn't have any strength," says Dan. "When we came to Key Bridge near mile four he could barely crank it. Then I noticed the front wheel axel had come loose and the wheel was pressing up against his brake. He'd been rolling this thing all that way with the brake on and was worn out!" One of the officials on the course was able to fix the wheelchair, but by then Dan and Zach were way behind the other wheelchair racers, and had been overtaken by the multitude of runners. Another problem was getting up—and down—the hills. "Typically you roll down one hill and can get halfway up the next with little effort," says Dan. "But Zach was apprehensive about getting up any speed going downhill, which is half the battle. It was much more physically demanding for us to go uphill with no momentum from the downhill." The time on the course also took its toll on Dan and Zach. For someone who was used to rolling through marathon courses in two hours, Dan was feeling it. "I found it's harder on you to crank slowly for six hours than it is to crank fast for two hours," he says. Now near the end of the course, after all the other wheelchair racers had finished, Zach was struggling even more.

The final mile of the course takes the athletes past Arlington

National Cemetery and up one more hill to the finish at the Marine Corps War Memorial. "We got to the bottom of the hill leading up to the finish and Zach was completely done," recalls Dan. "He slowed down and looked at me and shook his head. I knew that waiting for him at the top were his mother, sister, and girlfriend, and I said to myself that he was going up that hill come hell or high water! I don't usually wear my prosthetic leg when I race—it weighs eight pounds—but I had put it on for this race in case I had to get out of the my chair to offer him assistance. So, I got out, grabbed the front of my chair with one hand and put my other hand on his back and pushed him up the hill. When we got to within thirty yards of the finish line I gave him one more push and he did the rest. He was so happy he literally cried. After that you couldn't wipe the grin off his face. I think it gave him a sense that after all that, he could do anything, and that's why it was my best race. I've had much faster times, but it was because of him and because I was a part of it."

According to Dan, losing his leg was the best thing that ever happened to him. "It opened so many doors and changed my whole life. I've been able to travel and race all over the US and Europe, and it brought me back to my beloved Marines where I am able to coach the kids in the USMC Wounded War Regiment. To be able to show these kids that it's not the end of the world to come home wounded—that if I can do it they can do it—is the best job someone can have." On the Wounded War Regiment emblem there is a slogan in Latin. Translated, it means "Still in the Fight." "It's great to sit back and watch these kids," says Dan. "They lose their arms and their legs but they just don't quit. Like the slogan says, they are still in the fight." And so is Dan O'Connor.

Running Tip: "For future athletes who plan to race hand crank wheelchairs, the advice is train, train, train. Building upper body strength, mastering the gears to use in different situations, and channeling your power into an efficient shifting rhythm are the keys."

Kim Jones

After Kim Jones became a high school state champion in the mile, she didn't run a step for another six years. In between she attended college and settled down to raise a family in Spokane, Washington. But on a spring morning many years later on the streets of the city, her running career was resurrected; after she was found in the gutter.

Kim's story leading up to that point began a year earlier in front of the TV. "I hadn't run at all since high school and was sitting in my pajamas watching the '81 Bloomsday race," she recalls. One of the largest and most prestigious races in the country, Lilac Bloomsday attracts nearly 50,000 entrants every year during the first Sunday in May. Since its inaugural run in 1977, over a million runners have navigated the 12K (7.4 miles) course that weaves back and forth across the scenic Spokane River Gorge and climbs Doomsday Hill. "Watching the race inspired me to run the following year, and my goal was to run the entire distance without having to walk."

Fast forward one year—another year without any running—and Kim entered the race as planned. "Pretty much I was starting from scratch," she says. "I hadn't run a step before the race and I ran the entire distance, but it hurt. It was really a struggle. I plopped down on the curb with every muscle aching, and this woman sat down beside me and we started talking. She had this lovely accent. I told her how I ran the entire distance without having to walk and then I finally asked her how she did. She said, 'I'm Anne Audain and I won the race!' Anne gave me some words of encouragement, and I trained for a year for the next Bloomsday, where I finished eighth and won prize money.

I became an elite runner that day. Anne would later tell people that she was the one who found me, and that she found me in the gutter."

What Kim found was that gift of running that had lain dormant all those years. She also found a coach who put her on an elite training regimen that turned the one-time state champion miler into a world-class marathoner. In the years that followed, Kim would attain the number three ranking in the world in the marathon, be inducted into the Road Runners Club of America Hall of Fame, and become one of the greatest runners in history at the 26.2-mile distance. But a win in her hometown race had always eluded her, and time was running out.

"Winning Bloomsday had been my dream going all the way back to 1982 when I was sitting in the gutter with Anne Audain," she says. "I really wanted to win it for the townspeople but I never finished higher than fifth." As the years went by without that first-place finish, the thought of not winning became a burden to Kim. "There was one year I had signed up and planned to run and there was so much pressure that after warming up I just turned around, went the other way, and did a long run."

Leading up to the 1997 Bloomsday Run, Kim was running well and had developed a good base of speed to go with her high mileage. "I was on a roll in my racing," she says. "I went on the track that spring and focused on training for the Olympic Trials in the 5K. Running track races and workouts sparked my desire to run hard and gave me another gear. And racing in shorter distances at a faster pace carried over to Bloomsday. My last long run before Bloomsday was thirteen days before the race when I ran the Boston Marathon," something she says she wouldn't recommend to anyone leading up to an important race. "At Boston it was a windy day and I didn't beat myself up, but my legs were tired and I was mentally drained. But I had just turned thirty-nine and it would almost certainly be my last chance to win Bloomsday after I had tried so many times before, so I decided to go for it and see what happened."

Having less than two weeks to recover from a major

marathon was just one of the challenges facing Kim the day of the race. "My legs were heavy," she says, "the competition was really strong, and I was given bib number one, which put more pressure on me. Then fifteen minutes before the start I took my racing flats out of my backpack and realized they were two different shoes. One shoe was red and white and size eight, and the other was purple and white and size nine. At least they fit all right, and thank goodness they were both racing flats. Most importantly, I had a left shoe and a right shoe."

At Bloomsday the elite women are able to start fifteen minutes before the elite men and the 50,000 other runners. Therefore, Kim knew it would be a tactical race in which a woman would not be able to hide in the crowd of runners or tuck in behind a male runner to be pulled along for a fast time. She was also grateful for a relatively slow start since she wasn't sure how her legs would react. "A local runner I knew took off faster than I thought she was capable of running for very long, so we all let her go," she recalls, but the pace of 5:28 per mile for the first two miles was very slow. "An American, Carol Zajac, was leading our pack and started picking up the pace. She was a 1,500-meter runner and had been running well all year, and she was someone who could win the race." As the pace dropped to 5:10 per mile pace, the pack easily caught and passed the woman who had gone out to the early lead.

By then the lead pack had dwindled to eight runners, including Gladys Ondeyo of Kenya, Olympian Martha Tenoria from Ecuador, and three Russians, along with Kim. "I was already tired and wanted to take a breather and slip behind the pack," she says. "In the past I always backed off a little at such times, or took a rest here or there, but I knew I had to stick with the leaders and stay in the moment if I wanted to win." When Kim talks about "staying in the moment," she means putting aside negative thoughts and staying intensely focused on the task at hand. For her, "It is a magical place where my mind and body work in perfect sync, and movements seem to flow without conscious effort."

From the fans who had followed her career, Kim heard

encouragement all along the course, none more uplifting than the chorus she heard at three miles. "There was a high school track team working the aid station," she recalls, "and they were chanting my name, 'Kim Jones, Kim Jones, Kim Jones,' as I ran by, and it really lifted my spirits. I felt proud to be recognized by the young, up-and-coming athletes in Spokane. They gave me the encouragement I needed to persevere and stay with the pack at that part of the race."

Doomsday Hill is the infamous half-mile incline beginning at four and a half miles on the course, but it is an obstacle the hometown girl knew better than anyone else in the race. "I had done my hill training on that hill every week," she says, "so I was very comfortable with it even though we were racing hard. When we hit Doomsday Hill, Carole just took off. I wanted to stay with the pack because I was hurting, but she was running strong and I knew I had to go with her. Just before we crested the hill, I noticed Carole was hunching her shoulders and landing hard and her feet stayed on the ground a bit too long. I think all racers know when their competition is faltering a little bit, and she was losing her form. I knew then I had to make my move if I wanted to win the race. I've told others that if you make your move you have to make it count, so I just put my head down and went. With two miles still to go in the race it was going to be a long move. Carole followed me, but I had already put about eight seconds on her."

Throughout her career, Kim's asthma always seemed to keep her at a disadvantage. Her recent training and racing on the track, however, taught her that she could push a little harder, as she did that day. "Being a marathoner over the years, I was always taking a step back because of my asthma," she says. "I never pushed myself to the point where I went beyond my threshold because I was worried I'd have an asthma attack. My approach was just to stay in my comfort zone. But I knew from running those track races that as long as I didn't go all out for a long period of time, I could tolerate that higher level of exertion.

"I took a peek behind me each time I turned a corner to make sure I kept that distance, fighting the headwind alone as

I worked toward the finish line. Carole stayed eight seconds behind me right to the final uphill into the finish. I wasn't sure how my legs were going to hold up on that last hill because they were feeling that hilly Boston course from just thirteen days earlier, but as I ran toward the finish line, I began to realize I was about to win my hometown race. It was the biggest moment of my career. I savored every single step, hearing the crowd roaring just for me. The crowd seemed bigger and louder than the ones in New York and Boston—at least they did to me that day.

"Crossing the finish line was the most exhilarating moment of my life. So many people in Spokane had followed my long and eventful fifteen-year career, and I really wanted to win it for them. But the most rewarding part was seeing my daughter there with tears in her eyes. She had been with me throughout my entire career and was the only one who really knew how much it meant to me." In the days and weeks to come, parents and teachers would tell Kim that little girls were running around with sunglasses, their hair in ponytails, and wearing two different shoes, just like Kim. "I was a superstar for a while, and that was really cool."

Shortly after her win at Bloomsday, Kim retired from road racing. "It was pretty much the icing on the cake," she says. "I had some great races in my career, but at Bloomsday I never really had a great race; I just never gave myself a chance. The fact that I was able to overcome so much adversity, with what it meant to the townspeople, and to see the tears in my daughter's eyes at the finish, really made it the most special race of my life."

Running Tip: "Go into a race with a prerace strategy and adjust the plan if needed as the race goes on, and try always to stay in the moment."

Cathy O'Brien

"My son said I should talk about one of my Olympic races because that's what people want to hear, but I kept coming back to this one," says Cathy O'Brien. "This one was special to me for a few reasons. It's almost not a great story to tell because it was so simple, it was like I just turned on a switch and it was effortless." If Cathy's race was indeed "effortless," it was all the more remarkable because it resulted in a world record! Or *did* it?

Growing up, the future two-time Olympian's first love was playing the violin, which she began in second grade. But once in high school her music played second fiddle to her running, which eventually caught the interest of college recruiters. "I had many offers and went to the University of Oregon, but I only stayed a semester because it wasn't a great fit for me," she says. "After that I really didn't compete collegiately. I kind of foundered a bit because I wasn't on a team, and I decided to give up my eligibility to focus on trying to qualify for the Olympics. I was still running, but I really wasn't competing too much." With a strategy she would embrace throughout much of her career, Cathy kept a light competitive schedule, but incorporated several long runs into her weekly training regimen. And she did it without a coach. "I had a coach in high school who had given me a strong foundation of how to train and it seemed like it worked. Then I was married at age twenty and my husband was also a runner. Between the two of us we figured out what I should do. Who knew if it was all right or wrong, but in the end that's what it was."

Whatever it was, worked, as Cathy earned a place on the 1988 Olympic team in the marathon, a spot she would hold again four years later. "It was pretty much after 1988 that I started pursuing running as a profession," she recalls. "I was sort of new to the road racing scene, so when I went to races I would view each one just as important as the next one. At that time I was in between the two Olympic marathons, and those were good years for me. I was young and really didn't have a lot of miles on my legs. I began training at least 100 miles a week, and liked to go out and run twenty-plus miles and medium-long runs of sixteen. That was one of my things. I wanted my weekly mileage to be based more on single long runs as opposed to breaking it up into five miles and eight miles, for example. And I really didn't do much track work in my career at all. I would do longer intervals like 5x2 miles at 5-minute pace, and then do that four or five times. Or I would do 8 x 1 mile or long tempo runs."

In August of 1989 Cathy entered the Bobby Crim 10-Mile Run, a race through the streets of Flint, Michigan that has been a favorite of elite runners around the world since its inception. Launched in 1977 by Michigan House Speaker Bobby Crim and his assistant Lois Craig, the race is organized by the Crim Fitness Foundation which is committed to improving community health in Flint and beyond through physical activity and nutrition programs. The race currently draws more than 10,000 participants as part of the Crim Festival of Races. "I wasn't racing every weekend," she says, "and that was my race for the month. I really cared about it. I went out with the attitude that not only did I want to try and win it, but I really wanted to run super fast."

Cathy remembers Lisa Rainsberger as her main competition going into that race, but it appears once the race began, it didn't matter who was running against her. "I went to the lead and held it and kept building and building on it," she recalls. "It didn't feel like I was racing against any other competitors. I knew I had men running with me and around me, but I wasn't focusing on who was where in terms of the women competitors because I was in a zone that lasted from the first mile to the last mile. I remember clicking off splits in the low five minutes and thinking, 'Wow!'"

Cathy admits she took a risk going out as fast as she

did, but credits her training with providing the courage and determination to maintain that pace. "I really raced sparingly, so a lot of my confidence came from the workouts I did," she says. "Quite often I would go into a race with such internal confidence—not so much that I'm going to beat someone— but just knowing how strong I was and knowing what I was capable of. In this race that feeling never went away. It's kind of a simple feeling but it doesn't always happen that way. I had tons of training runs and workouts that were mind-boggling. I would run some amazing times because there was no pressure, it was just running, and that was the feeling I had in this race."

Cathy didn't know where Lisa or the other female competitors were as she approached the finish, but she felt far enough in the lead that sprinting to the line was not necessary. Even without a finishing sprint, Cathy was still able to run the fastest 10-mile road race ever by a woman: a world record time of 51:47. "I didn't know what the world record was for ten miles, but pretty soon after I finished people told me that was the case," she recalls. "I wasn't thinking about setting a record; it didn't cross my mind. Number one when you're in race is to win, and I certainly had tons of respect for Lisa because she was great at those distances. I just remember thinking that the pace was really fast and I hoped I could keep it up."

Then came some bad news: it wasn't a world record after all. Why? Cathy had gone off course. "I was ahead and toward the end of the race, maybe the last mile or so, I was following the lead police vehicle where they directed me. After I finished I learned at some point they had misdirected me and the runners behind me. I had finished, won the race, set a world record, the whole thing was great, and then they said, 'It can't be a world record because you didn't follow the right course.' So that put a damper on it. It's hard not to remember the range of emotions associated with it; the whole experience was like being on a roller coaster." Race officials spent three hours remeasuring the course and gave the result to Cathy right before she left town: not only would her world record stand, but the course she ran was actually *longer* than ten miles!

"For my mind to keep coming back to this race after all these years shows it was kind of special," she says. It was because of how I felt when I was running it. It was like one of those days I only had before in training where I just felt amazing and incredible and effortless like I could keep going and going. It was pure joy to put that kind of feeling and effort together in a race. I not only came away with a world record, but I came away feeling like I really got the most out of myself on that day. It's something I don't think I'll ever forget."

With her competitive running career over, Cathy has time again for the violin. She gives lessons in her studio and at a local school, but still makes time for a daily ten-mile run. Or maybe it's a little *longer* than ten miles…

Running Tip: "I still love running. Find joy in your daily running and be confident that your work will pay off for you in a race. It's definitely transferable. You don't have to look for the latest training advice in a magazine. Just go out and put in the miles, keep it simple, and enjoy it, and you will be successful in your race."

Heather Gannoe

How can someone's best race be one they never even finished? "It all depends on what you put into it," says Heather Gannoe. And if there's anyone who knows about effort, it's Heather, who holds a BA in exercise science and works as a personal trainer, a wellness coach, and an ACSM Certified Health Fitness Specialist. "I have an undying passion to motivate people to become active and healthy," she says. And that includes herself. "Every day I try to do something different to increase my strength and endurance because I love to push myself, I welcome the challenge." It comes as no surprise, therefore, that the name of her website is "Relentless Forward Commotion."

Obviously, anyone who fits Heather's description would put a race called the Ultra Beast on their bucket list, especially those living near Killington, Vermont where the race is held each September. What makes the race so challenging, besides being slightly longer than a marathon? Let's start with the obstacles. "You have to do some crazy things out there," says Heather. Here's a partial list:

Ditch jump
Fire jump
Cargo net climb
Rope climb
Trench crawl
Barbed wire crawl
Sled pull
Tractor pull
Tyrolean traverse

Sandbag carry
7-foot wall
Slippery wall
Monkey bars
40-degree swim

"But most of all you climb," she says. The first fourteen miles are straight up a mountain." And once a runner conquers the mountain and navigates through the jumps, the crawls, the barbed wire, and over the walls, they have to go back and do it all over again! Of course, the race doesn't take just anybody. According to their website, "For your own safety and for the competitive nature of the event, you will have to apply for acceptance." That means submitting a resume of your running history and a paragraph about why in the world you would want to subject yourself to their beastly marathon-length obstacle course. Heather's experience with marathons, mud runs, trail races, and triathlons, along with a convincing written argument for her inclusion, gained her entry into the 2012 race.

So, how does one train for the Ultra Beast? "Besides doing a lot of hiking, I looked for anything else I could do that would push me to get stronger but also make me uncomfortable; a lot of nontraditional training." For example, after each half-mile run on a trail, she would stop and do plyometric exercises (that is, exercises that use explosive movements to train muscles to exert maximum force in a short amount of time, such as pushups and jumping lunges). Along with her regular running routine, she also added box jumps, burpees (or squat thrusts), stair climbs, and hill runs while carrying a log. In case that wasn't enough, she also set up her own mini obstacle course. And speaking of obstacles, it surely didn't help when three weeks before the race she suffered through bouts of bronchitis and tonsillitis.

"When I got to the starting line I was terrified," she recalls. "They don't publish a course map so it's always a little scary going into a situation where you don't know what you are about to face. But just being surrounded by all the energy of the small community of runners was very reassuring. After a minute or two I was really excited to be there, and after a minute on the racecourse I felt fine." Despite the nasty collection of impediments placed in her way, Heather's main obstacle was getting up—and down—that mountain. "Very few of those first fourteen miles to the top are on an actual trail," she says. "You go through knee-high grass, waist-high grass, and then a forest. But one of the most painful parts of the event is the downhill because it's steep, it's slippery, and you're constantly falling. It hurt. It hurt a lot."

Nevertheless, according to Heather, "That first full lap was awesome. I couldn't believe how great I felt, and how many people I was passing. Someone even said I looked like a mountain goat. And on one of the obstacles I climbed to the top of the rope and rang the bell when so many others couldn't." Heather finished the first of two laps in a respectable 5 hours and 49 minutes. It wasn't until she arrived at the transition area that her problems began.

"By the time I arrived at the transition area I was soaking wet, cold, hungry, and exhausted," she says. "The spectators all looked so warm and comfy, so I sat down and it was probably the worst thing I could have done. I started second-guessing myself. So many had already quit; grown men who I knew were physically fit had dropped out after that first lap. That voice in the back of my head was so loud saying, 'Just quit, you did good, you came in before so many other people on that lap. Get warm, get some food.' It was a mental game I was playing with myself, and a half hour went by in the blink of an eye. Finally I decided I would never forgive myself if I don't at least try, so I changed my shoes and shirt, ate some food, and went back out."

Runners are allowed to rest in the transition area for as long as they want, but for their health and safety, there is a time limit for completing the course. "I was really happy that I kept going and did not quit," Heather recalls, "but unfortunately, I think that half hour at the transition did me in. After another eleven miles some volunteers pulled me off the course due to the time cutoff, so I didn't get to finish. Including that first lap I had been on the course for over eleven hours.

"The Ultra Beast was my first DNF, but also the race I'm most proud of," she says. "It was the hardest thing I've ever done in my life, and, after going through a period of post-race depression, I realized it was the greatest thing I've ever done in my life too. Why? Because I really surprised myself. I was able to do a lot more than I thought I could, and that was such a rewarding feeling for me. I learned that if you are confident in yourself and your training, and rely on your mental strength, it takes you to another level and there is nothing out there that you can't do if you keep pushing yourself."

And just how confident is Heather now? "I have a score to settle with that mountain," she says. "Next year I'll know what I'm up against and I'll hopefully beat it. And then for me DNF won't be 'Did Not Finish'; it will be 'Did Not *Fail*'"

Running Tip: "Embrace the bad times. That horrible feeling you get in training or in a race? Realize it is making you stronger. Sometimes you just need to stop and think why you are doing it, and the answer is that it's something you love to do. So, make the best of it."

Don Kardong

As a 6'3" basketball player in high school, Don Kardong knew more about running a fast break than he did about running cross-country. "I watched distance races and it looked like people just jogged for a long time and then sprinted at the end," he says amusingly. "Then one day our cross-country coach went to my basketball coach and asked him to talk me into going out for cross-country. He thought I would be a good runner." The coach was right, but it didn't happen overnight. Though no college recruiter believed he would be anything special as a runner, one race finally gave him the confidence he needed to believe in himself. That race would eventually pave the way to an Olympic berth and reserve him a spot in the Distance Running Hall of Fame.

Don began to make progress on his high school cross-country team when he overcame his initial misguided perceptions of how to run a distance race. "Once I figured you're supposed to actually run hard the whole time and then run really fast at the end, my performance improved quite a bit," he says. "By the end of the season I was number one on our team." Once Don graduated to attend Stanford, his basketball days were over, but his enthusiasm for running convinced him to join the freshman cross-country team as a non-scholarship student athlete.

"We had a freshmen-only cross-country team in college," he says. "I think if I had to step up to college varsity competition right away, I wouldn't have had the guts. I had a good freshman year and could actually think about stepping up to varsity as a sophomore, but it really wasn't until my senior year that I was really fit and running well." Despite being fit, Don often had trouble with something most of us suffer through on a regular basis: side stitches. "I would often get them on a hilly course," he recalls, like the course where the conference cross-country championship was held that year. "At Washington State it was a hilly golf course we ran on and I developed a stitch and ended up finishing about tenth. I was real disappointed after that, but I did qualify to go to the nationals in Williamsburg, Virginia."

At the time, Don and his Stanford teammates were training twice a day, five days a week, and covering about 80-90 miles. "Our longest run was fifteen miles, and we had two pretty intense days of speed work each week," he says. "We did mile and half-mile repeats on a golf course and the shorter intervals on the soccer field."

Upon arriving at the site of the NCAA Championship meet in Williamsburg, Don liked what he saw. "It was a perfect course for me because there were almost no hills of any kind. Real flat, mostly on a dirt road out in the woods, so I wasn't going to have any trouble with my side stitch. A day before the race we went over the course and the start was across this big field for maybe a quarter mile before it narrowed to that dirt road. Basically there were going to be hundreds of runners lined up across this big field and, as my coach said to me, everybody is going to want to get to that road first. He said, 'You're going to have to be in the hunt, but don't overdo it because most of those guys are going to run too fast and not be able to sustain it.' He told me the race would be fast no matter what, but if I could come through the first mile in about 4:30 and no faster than that, I would be in good shape."

Sure enough, just as the coach predicted, the mass of runners sprinted all-out across the field toward the narrow dirt road. "I tried to position myself farther back but still far enough ahead where I didn't get totally buried," says Don. "I remember coming through the mile and they called out '4:31.' It was exactly what we wanted to do; I thought, 'I got this thing in the bag.' I was probably in twenty-fifth place at that point. So now we were on that dirt road and as a tall runner, a flat course works best for me. I've never been a good hill runner up or down, but on a flat course I can stretch out and make use of my height. What I remember is that I started to pass all the guys that beat me at the conference meet. I don't remember when I moved into the top five, I just remember steadily moving up through the crowd, passing people who had gone out too fast."

Up ahead in front was the runner who had gone out faster than anyone else, although he was one of the few who could sustain such a punishing pace. The University of Oregon's Steve Prefontaine ("Pre") was on his way to becoming the legend and cult figure he remains today, eventually winning three NCAA cross-country championships and holding every American record from the 2,000 to the 10,000. He would die in a car accident four years later. "I had this special moment at about 4 miles," says Don, "where I caught Pre, who was leading. He had a clear break from the rest of the crowd. When I saw that it was him I was pretty excited that we were going to have some kind of battle over the final mile or so, but when he heard me coming, he glanced back and then threw it into another gear (Don laughs) and just took off. He just revved it up to a new level, but I remember just being so pumped that I had moved up to contend for first."

Near the end of the 6-mile race Don was passed by another runner, but held on to finish a strong third. "I just remember I was slightly disappointed that I hadn't been able to stay with Pre and then got passed, but thinking that I was the third best collegiate runner in the country was quite a thrill. It felt relatively easy to move up through the crowd, and I have to say that's probably as good as I have ever felt in a race. I remember some of the runners who I lost to at the conference meet but who I beat in this race told me they couldn't believe I was tenth at the conference meet and third at the national meet. I would say they were a little surprised.

"Psychologically it was a big race for me because it gave me the sense that I could be competitive with the best runners in the country," he says, "which eventually got me to thinking about the Olympics. It was at that point I realized that on a good day, I could make an Olympic team, and it was such an important race for me for that reason. I'd had some good races up to that point, but it was that cross-country race that really gave me a lot of confidence. When I was tenth in my conference I didn't think of myself as being a contender nationally. But when I was able to turn it around at the national meet with all the best collegiate runners in the country there, it was a big deal for me. After that when I would have a bad race, I would remember that I was able to do it on that day, and that I should be able to do it again."

Don is the founder and race director of the Lilac Bloomsday 12K run in Spokane, Washington. In 1976, he earned a spot on the US Olympic team and finished fourth in the marathon at the Montreal Olympics.

Running Tip: "Channel your enthusiasm. You don't need to whip yourself up in a race. You need to channel it so you don't do something stupid early on. You want to use that energy but you don't want it to carry you over a cliff."

Jessica Crate

Jessica Crate (left) at the Triathlon World Championship

Jessica Crate was on a roll. Leading up to the 2011 Boston Marathon she had won the women's race in both the Gasparilla Classic and the St. Petersburg Rock 'n' Roll Half Marathon, and had finished third (31st overall) in the Walt Disney World Marathon with a time of 2:51. Then at Boston, running with her coach and training partner, she was on pace to achieve her dream of posting an Olympic Trials qualifying time—until she reached mile fourteen. "I stepped wrong around a water stop to avoid some other runners and felt this pain shooting all the way up to my neck," she says. "My foot felt like it was on fire and I didn't know what was wrong. But I just had to keep going.

Despite what felt like daggers in my foot, I told myself I was going to finish that race." It wasn't until Jessica was wheeled to the medical tent after crossing the finish line that she learned she had run the final twelve miles of the Boston Marathon on a broken foot.

Remarkably her finishing time was just over three hours, although that was of little comfort to her. "I ran a 3:04 which requalified me for Boston, but it shattered my dreams of running in the Olympic Trials. It was devastating. I was six weeks in a boot cast and thought about all that hard work and realized there was no way I would be able to qualify for the Olympic Trials that year." Fortunately for Jessica, as one window closed, a few others opened. "I began physical therapy and still couldn't run, so I started biking and swimming like a maniac," she says, and that was enough to get her competitive juices flowing again. Although her foot was still not completely healed, Jessica became reacquainted with the triathlon. "It was an event I had dabbled in before," she says. "When I was finally able to run, it was in the back of my mind that my foot could break again, but I had to get over that negative mentality. I chose the sprint triathlons (half-mile swim/12-mile bike/5K run) because by then I could handle the shorter run segment." Then a funny thing happened: Jessica started winning them!

Soon she received a letter from USA Triathlon informing her she had qualified for the age group nationals that August. That was the good news. The bad news was that the race would be run at the "Olympic" distance (mile swim/25 mile bike/10K run). "I hadn't done more than twelve miles on the bike, or more than a half mile in the pool, or more than three miles in my run," she says. "I was only running maybe once or twice a week." But to her, the decision to accept the coveted invitation was a no-brainer.

"So I went to age group nationals and had a really bad beginning," she recalls. "During the swim my fingernail got snapped off and every stroke was brutal. I finished that segment back in 60th place, but I told myself I wasn't going to quit. Then I really hammered the bike stage and was in 32nd place at the start of the run." Jessica's foot, still not fully healed, was sore as she ran the final leg of the triathlon, but evidently it didn't hold her back. "I just ran and was passing people but had no idea what place I was in. I was told later that people following me online with the USA Triathlon tracker could see my dot moving quickly through the course. Then within the last four hundred yards I passed one more girl before I crossed the finish line." Jessica didn't realize it then, but that final burst was critical. By finishing in 18th place, she secured the final qualifying spot for the 2012 age group Triathlon World Championship in Auckland, New Zealand. "I realized breaking my foot at Boston was a pivotal moment. I never would have entered those triathlons—and qualified for the World Championship—if I hadn't broken my foot."

Another window that opened up for her was a new job. "With my foot still trying to heal, I was approached by a friend who gave me a video about a nutraceutical product." Impressed with how the product helped her recovery and her performance, she now works for the company as a distributor. Jessica also finds the time to coach athletes as a certified Natural Running Instructor and helps run a charity she cofounded called Giving Athletics, Inc., whose goal is to inspire social change through athletic participation. Her website jessicacrate.com has more information on this charity and on each of the other facets of her career.

Now completely healthy and back to winning races, Jessica has a goal of qualifying for the Olympic Trials marathon in 2016. When she looks back to her Boston Marathon and her broken foot, she says, "It was a point in my life where I was literally brought down to ground zero. I realized everything that I planned and worked for was not going to happen, but eventually it all worked out for the better."

Running Tip: "I'm a proponent of natural running, and I would tell runners that it doesn't matter what type of shoes they wear or what type of runner they are; if they can get down to basics with natural running they can conquer any distance while being injury free."

Ryan Lamppa

©Swift County Mo...

Ryan Lamppa was not supposed to be a factor in the state championship 100-yard dash; the longer sprints were his specialty. He knew the favorite was undefeated and had more raw speed, which meant when running side by side, Ryan would most likely come out the loser. So if Ryan wanted to give a good showing and maybe even win, there seemed only one option: he had to get the best start he ever had in his life.

As spokesperson for Running USA, a nonprofit devoted to promoting the sport of running and advancing its growth, Ryan can handle any question or request about running. Indeed, part of the organization's mission is to be a resource for anyone who wants to find out more about the sport. Their annual "State of the Sport" reports, for example, feature road racing statistics, industry trends, and core runner profiles.

Back in 1977, Ryan Lamppa's runner profile was one of a quarter miler with a good chance to repeat as state champion in that distance. When the state meet began in June, Ryan was also expected to do well in the 220. Ryan at first didn't give the 100-yard dash much thought. If anything he would be an "also-ran" in that event. "In my senior year in high school I had qualified for the state meet in the 100, 220, and 440," says Ryan. "I had won the 440 the previous year and I figured I might win the 440 again and probably place high in the 220. But the 100 was more of a crapshoot. A guy named Pat Stone had finished second in the 100 the previous year. He was the favorite, and if memory serves me he was undefeated that year."

The favorite, as expected, beat Ryan in the preliminary

race Friday night, and Ryan was just happy to qualify for the final. His main focus would be the 440 and 220 races. "I wasn't that fast and I wasn't that great of a starter," says Ryan. "I just wanted to make the final in the 100 and had no expectations; whatever happened, happened." Still, with the 100 being the first final of the meet the next day, Ryan wanted to do as best he could in order to gain some momentum going into his other two races. He knew he had put in the work during the year, now he just had to "dream big" as he puts it. "So it got me thinking, how can I beat him? Pat had more raw speed than I did, so I thought if we're even after the start he's going to beat me again. So my thought was, 'It's the start!' If I came out even at the start or behind, he's going to beat me. But if I could get out of the starting blocks before Pat, I would at least have a chance of beating him.

"I had the same starter for all my preliminary races on Friday night and I was very cognizant to get his cadence down. And before the 100 finals the next day they held the 120-yard hurdles, and I remember listening to the starter in that race too and counting it in my head. I thought I'd have to come as close to a false start as possible or I wasn't going to win."

Warming up before the 100 final, Ryan recalls feeling good and loose with no anxiety about the outcome. He drew lane five beside Pat Stone in lane four. "I told myself to try and anticipate the gun," says Ryan. "I don't doubt that if they had those sensors in my starting blocks like they do now, I would probably be close to being too fast out of the blocks (and considered a false start). When the gun went off and I left the blocks and came up running, I couldn't see anyone on either side of me. For a nanosecond I thought, 'Did I jump the gun?' but they didn't call us back. Once I got out and couldn't sense anyone to my left or to my right, my instincts were, 'I'm ahead!'

"So I'm out and I'm just bounding down the track on a beautiful June day in Minnesota. I remember flying down that track like I had never flown down it before, like I was being pulled in a vacuum. I don't recall feeling anyone near me in the race at all, and I can't think of another race where that ever happened. I don't even have a memory of feeling the track. I remember as the finish line was approaching I thought, 'Don't let up,' because I had a feeling I could win it, and I knew I was never going to have that moment again. It's just one of those things that came together so well from the start through the entire race and suddenly I crossed the line and realized, 'I've just won this!'"

Ryan's winning time of 9.9 seconds was the first time he ever broke the ten-second barrier. Pat Stone's second-place time was ten flat. "The start gave me the extra tenth," he says. "In the local paper there was a photograph of me with Pat right after we finished. He and I both had looks of shock on our faces. He had his hands on his hips and his look was like, 'What just happened?' I looked like a boy who just got a Christmas present that was totally unexpected but wonderful. If I had finished fourth or fifth I would have been happy. It was just one of those magic times when everything just lined up."

Full of confidence, Ryan went on to win both the 440 (in record time) and the 220. "The 100 win was the catalyst for what happened the rest of the day," he recalls. "I repeated as the 440 champion and my teammate was second. Then I came back ninety minutes later and won the 220, and my teammate was third. At the time I was the third or fourth Minnesotan to triple at the state meet. But that 100 set it all up. That was the one that was hardest to win. It has been thirty-six years and I still look back and think, 'How *did* that happen?' I had no expectations. I just wanted to do the best I could, and in this case it turned out I had the start of my life and that led to the other two titles. And I'm now part of Minnesota track history.

"But I know it wasn't just me. I had four other teammates who pushed me all year in every single meet, and I was very cognizant of that. I told my coach and my teammates that the gold medal in the 100 wasn't just mine. My teammate Jeff Eckhoff was second in the 440 and third in the 220, and I knew I made him better and he made me better. There was all that synergy of a team. That's why that medal has a very special place in my mind and my heart. I have a very vivid memory of all the trophies I have ever won in sports and that 100-yard gold medal means more to me than all the rest of them. If I had to keep only one, even though I was a two-time winner in the 440 and the state record holder, the medal for the 100 is the one I'd keep. And it was the one that was most unexpected, too.

"So for me, the combination of being at the state meet, being a senior, having no expectations of winning, having the best start of my life, being in that zone, my teammate pushing me, and going down the track like in a dream, it was a near perfect race I was never able to replicate." And, according to Ryan, the knowledge of what can be accomplished with hard work, good teammates, and good performance, has carried over to other parts of his life ever since. "Even to this day I think back to that moment. But it wasn't just a one-off thing. What happened there also transcended into other parts of my life. It was more than just that state title. It was part of the process of how I have gone through my life of working hard and dreaming big. It's one of those things that got me to where I am right now."

Running Tip: "Train hard, have passion, and dream big. And it's not just about running but a philosophy for other parts of life too."

Kathrine Switzer

Kathrine Switzer at the start of the Athens Marathon

"You know there are times when you run a race and you know from the beginning that you're in deep trouble? At the Athens Marathon, I knew right from the beginning." Throughout her career as a driving force for creating opportunities in sports for women, Kathrine Switzer has been associated with the Boston Marathon. In 1967, registered as K. Switzer, she became the first woman to officially enter the all-male race. Consequently, she also became the first woman that race officials attempted to physically remove from the race, once they discovered her true identity. That attempt failed, but thirty-four years later she was nearly forced from another marathon—this time through no one's fault but her own.

In 490 BC, a Greek courier named Phidippides ran 26 miles from Marathon to Athens with word of his country's victory over the Persians. Reportedly he declared, "Rejoice, we conquer," before collapsing and dying. Whether the courier story is fact or fiction, the Greek victory was itself a significant part of world history. And no marathon, including Boston, is enveloped in as much history as the Athens Marathon, which commemorates the twenty-six-mile distance from the Plains of Marathon to the Greek capital. Kathrine was in Germany in 1972 covering the Olympic Games for the *New York Daily News* when she considered entering the Athens Marathon. "While in Europe I was invited to run in a lot of male-only races to break the gender barrier," she recalls. "It was an amazing experience and I was always welcome." When she contacted the Greek Athletic Federation for permission to enter their all-male marathon, however, she was denied. At least Kathrine had a chance to tour part of the course before she returned home. "I went down to the beach at Marathon and found the great burial mound," she says, referring to the hallowed location where 192 Athenian soldiers from the Battle of Marathon are buried. "When the Athenian soldiers defeated the Persians, it was a huge victory, considered one of the turning points in history and one of the battles that changed the face of the world because it saved what was then the fledgling idea of a democracy. The idea of a democracy was way out there, just like women's marathon running. I was upset that I never got to race the marathon. I didn't harbor any bitterness but I didn't forget."

Thirty-eight years later was a special anniversary for that race, and by then women had been allowed to compete. "When the 2,500th anniversary came along I said I was going to run that race," says Kathrine. "It was the anniversary of the Battle of Marathon and therefore the history of the marathon. But I hadn't run a marathon in thirty-two years. So I trained for eighteen months, ran a mountain race in New Zealand and some half marathons, and decided to enter."

Putting a kink in the final preparations for her first marathon in three decades was the need for Kathrine to write a speech she had been invited to give in Athens before the race. "When I arrived in Athens I was really tired and jet lagged and I hadn't done some of the last-minute training I wanted to do. So I went to the starting line and told myself to just take it easy, and to walk some of the race," she recalls. "The night before, they honored me and gave me an elite bib so I found myself on the elite starting line with the Kenyans and alongside America's Joan Benoit. Joan said, 'I can't believe you're running this,' and I said, 'I can't believe I'm running this either.' And off we went."

The race begins in the town of Marathon, and soon after the start takes the runners past the sacred ground Kathrine had visited years before. "After the start you make a loop around the burial mound of the soldiers," she says. "At that point scores if not hundreds of runners stopped and took out their cell phones to take pictures of that magical spot because it's a shrine." After that photo session, runners faced a course that steadily rises in elevation for about thirty kilometers. "I remember on the way out to the start with a busload of people it became quieter and quieter because we could see that we were going down hills, and everybody knew we were eventually going to have to come *up* them.

"I was tired and dehydrated and it was hot," recalls Kathrine, after just a few miles into the race. "I had to walk for a little bit at the 5K mark to catch my breath because it was so hot, and then right after halfway my quads completely cramped. That had never happened to me before and I didn't even know how to deal with it. I remember there were many first aid guys along the course with red crosses pinned on the front of their windbreakers and they had cans that I presumed was some kind of numbing spray and people were running over to them and getting their legs and calves sprayed. I didn't know what it was but I said, 'I'm going to get some of that too,' so I asked them to spray my quads and then I stretched and walked."

Kathrine's husband, Roger, planned to meet her at the 30K point in the race to offer support, unaware of the struggle his wife had been going through and unaware he would be a target of her frustration. "I was really boohooing by then," she says.

"It was total self-doubt, the first time in my life I had total self-doubt that I could do it, and by that time it was all his (her husband's) fault! He put his jacket down for me to sit on to stretch and said, 'It wouldn't be the worst thing if you had to drop out,' and I said, 'It would too!' I've never dropped out of a race and I surely didn't want the first one to be the 2,500th anniversary of the marathon. I got up and hobbled off like Charlie Chaplin at the end of a film."

Even without having run the 26.2-mile distance in thirty-two years, the former winner of the New York City Marathon and Distance Running Hall of Fame inductee knew how to come back from difficult situations in any race, and that is what she did. "Sometimes it's good if you just stop and stretch and take a deep breath and say, 'Okay, look, you're not having a great day, just get through it.' At that point it still hurt like hell but I said to myself, 'Hey, I think you can do this,' and I started passing people. And then every mile, it was, 'You can do this.' And then there was that wonderful moment when all of a sudden you're coming down the last stretch and you could see and hear the crowd in the stadium and that *Zorba the Greek* music. We came in the stadium and the crowed was just unbelievable and it was the first time I ever cried at the end of a marathon; I just burst into tears." Finally crossing the finish line with a respectable time of 4:42, especially with all the walking she had done on the course, Kathrine felt a combination of relief and joy. "Oh my gosh, it's over. I did it!" she recalls thinking. "I was sixty-three years old having attempted something overwhelming after all those years and proving I could do it again. But this was so hard for me. As soon as I found Roger again I apologized. I was so horrible. I was taking everything out on him earlier in the race and I should have given him my finisher's medal."

Besides a finisher's medal, the race provided the sixty-three year-old with some new lessons to take back with her. "I learned so much late in life from that one event," she says. "I learned that I was totally vulnerable but that I could be invincible too. I learned that with the person I loved the most I could be totally cranky and unreasonable and I had never been cranky and unreasonable with Roger before. I learned not to goof off in training. I looked back at my training log and realized I never did my wall squats (the reason she says her quads tightened up), and I did most of my training on trails and not hard surfaces. And I also learned that to come back and run the race I've always wanted to run thirty-eight years after I was denied entry was just stunning. I felt incredibly privileged. And it was kind of the cycle of history. I've been running for fifty-three years and I've seen a lot of history, and I was a part of it. To then come full circle with this is just great. It's a brutal course but it is definitely a pilgrimage experience for runners. I was very happy just to be one of them."

Running Tip: "Everybody should try once to do a race better than they think they can do it. Most people are there for the event, the medal, the experience, and that's all good. But they should try to be better, because then they can look back on that part of their life and say, 'I gave it a good shot, I pushed myself, I tested my physical limits.' Learning to push yourself hard teaches you an awful lot about your inner self and about the world around you."

Anne Audain

"I always ran from the front," says New Zealand's Anne Audain, "it was just my nature. I always said that I don't want to run tactically. I don't want to be tripping over people." Nevertheless, when her coach instructed her *not* to run from the front in her 3,000-meter race at the 1982 Commonwealth Games, she promised to follow orders. After all, it was a windy day, and in such an important race why not let someone else be the frontrunner and do all the work? So after the twenty-five runners broke from the start and began the first of seven and a half laps, where was Anne? Out in front, naturally.

For the longest time, Anne had wanted no part of that race. She had been in the US dominating the new road racing circuit and believed her days of track racing were behind her. "In 1981 when I first visited the States, distance running opened up for women," she says. "Phil Knight put up money for the first professional road race, which I happened to win." There would be seventy-four more wins for Anne on American roads through the 1980s; overall, she would finish in the top three in ninety percent of her races.

Finishing a race, however, much less winning one, seemed out of the question thirteen years earlier when doctors performed complicated surgery on Anne's feet to remove bony growths. Once her casts were finally removed, she had to adjust to a new way of walking (the correct way), and there was uncertainty about what level she could attain in her running. Looking back, Anne credits that painful episode in her life as the reason for her frontrunner strategy. "I think my running style has a lot to do with the issues concerning my feet as a teenager," she says. "After I healed I became an up-on-my-toes runner, and I wanted to run smooth because my feet became uncomfortable if I had to keep switching the pace. If I'm not in a rhythm I'm a miserable runner, but by being out in front I can set my own rhythm; the pace is not being dictated to me by anyone else."

In the summer of 1982, while Anne was setting course records and winning every race she entered, she received a call from her old coach in New Zealand, John Davies. The Commonwealth Games, always following two years after the Olympics, were being held in neighboring Australia, and John wanted Anne to run the 3,000 meters. "I told John my track days were over," she recalls. "I didn't want to run track anymore. But he told me I had a great chance of winning a gold medal, something no New Zealand woman had ever done." Still Anne was hesitant. "At that point I was only ranked 9th in the commonwealth in the 3,000 and I was really not interested. I was doing really well in the US and having a blast. I kept saying 'no' to him." So her coach began talking about pride and family. "He really believed I could win a gold medal, and told me that I should do it for my country and for my parents. Finally I told him that if he could prove to me I could train for a 3,000 meter-race in the middle of competing in all the road races I was scheduled to run, I would do it."

Anne had never stopped doing track workouts as part of her training regimen for competing on the roads. If she decided to run the shorter, faster 3,000-meter distance, however, she would need to add more specialized workouts. "It would be a big deal switching from training to run 10Ks and ten milers to workouts that really weren't needed for those distances, so I had to have a bit more flexibility," she says. "When I finally agreed to run in the Commonwealth Games, John sent me a handwritten training schedule for the last nine weeks leading up to the 3,000 meter race (She still has it, and looks at it as we speak.) He goes through all the days and what he wants me to do each day, then for October 4th he writes 'gold medal day,' and for the day after that he writes 'go polish your medal.' That's the relationship we had. We had a great relationship as coach and athlete."

On October 4th athletes at the Commonwealth games faced "blustery conditions not conducive to fast times," according to the BBC announcer. Dressed in her all-black New Zealand uniform with the silver fern emblem, Anne was warming up when her coach approached. "I was on the practice track and John came over to me and said, 'Annie, it's very windy in the stadium and I know you like to run from the front, but you've got to promise me today that you can't do that. That's just not going to work. You're going to have to sit back and use your speed.' I told him I don't like to run that way, and he said, 'I just don't think you should lead the race,' so, I promised. Then I went into the stadium and realized just how windy it was."

Before the race, the runners had participated in a blind drawing to choose their starting positions, and Anne unfortunately picked the number one spot. "I chose the #1 card, which meant I was on the inside with twenty-four others out on the curve," she says. "What can happen is that when the gun goes off all those runners on the outside come streaming to the inside lane and you can get knocked off into the infield. If that happens to you, you get disqualified. So when the gun sounded, I just took off really fast to get out of trouble and nothing more, and found myself out in front. I thought, 'Oh no,' so I pulled back a little hoping someone would go past me, but no one did. Then I came around the home straight in front of the commentating booth where my coach was sitting, and all I was thinking was that I promised him I wouldn't get out in front. There I was in the first 200 meters—out in front!" Anne hesitated again, hoping someone would pass her and take the lead, but no one else was going to run into the wind. So she decided to do what she knew best—running from the front, forcing the pace, and challenging everyone else to keep up with her.

Anne ran each of the first two laps in sixty-nine seconds, which was fast even *without* a headwind. After another brisk lap she began to stretch the field, and only Wendy Smith of Great Britain, the record holder in the 3,000, could stay with her. As Anne recalls, "I thought she would just wait; that was her nature as a runner. She would just wait and then take a chance later. It really didn't bother me because the front was where I preferred to be. And every time we went down the back straight into the wind I could hear Wendy breathing really hard, and I thought she was breathing harder than I was." As the BBC announcer remarked, "Into the wind again on the back straight. You can see them actually bending into it!" Apparently, much of New Zealand was seeing it too. "It came on at 3:00 in the afternoon on a Monday," says Anne, "and I was told that there was so much publicity around the race that people all across New Zealand were lined up outside the stores that sold TVs watching it." Coincidentally, Anne also had a good view of her opponent behind her with the help of the Jumbotron at one end of the stadium. "I could look up and see her so I just felt like I was in control and that it was going to come down to a sprint. It was going to be me or her. I knew I had something left and was waiting for her to make a move."

With less than two laps remaining, Anne didn't realize she was on record pace. Her face betrayed no emotion as she continued to apply the pressure on the runner who tucked in behind her out of the wind. "I was able to maintain a consistent pace and stay focused," she recalls. "That was probably one of my biggest strengths as a runner. I was good at just getting into a rhythm and running lap after lap at the same pace. I don't remember the crowd and I don't remember the noise. I wasn't trained to do it, it just came naturally.

"Wendy came up on my shoulder just before the bell, and on that side we had a little tailwind, so I thought if she takes the lead now she would be in the lead going into the headwind on the back straight. I felt strong enough to certainly keep up with her, but she didn't go past. It wasn't a strong move, so I thought maybe she didn't have the confidence to do it. We went around the back straight one more time and she just tucked in behind me again as we went into the wind. Then as soon as we got the wind at our backs, she tried to pass one more time. I just happened to have it on that day." Instead of being passed in the final straight, Anne accelerated, leaving no doubt who was stronger.

"I finally did it," she remembers thinking as she crossed the finish line, arms outstretched, head tilted back, eyes gazing up at the sky. "It was just sheer relief that I finally did what my coach told me I possibly could. And I knew that everything I'd ever done before had led to that moment; it had all been worth it. And what made it even better was that I ran it my way, from the front. Even after I promised John that I wouldn't do that. I think I would never have forgiven myself if I had done it his way—I don't believe I would have won. I guess choosing that #1 card to start on the inside actually saved me."

In the end, the runner who broke a promise to her coach set a new record and became the first woman from New Zealand to win a gold medal in the Commonwealth Games. No doubt she was forgiven.

Running Tip: "If you want to improve in running you need to find a good coach. Ask around and get recommendations. Running and training is not complicated but you do need an individual plan for yourself."

Larry Rawson

Larry Rawson was elected to the Distance Running Hall of Fame not for his feet but for his voice. For more than three decades, the Emmy award-winning announcer has provided expert analysis on everything from the NCAA championships to the Boston Marathon to the Olympic Games. But long before "The Voice of Track and Field" ever entered the broadcast booth, he and three teammates made history on a cinder track in Philadelphia.

Larry's running career began at a school that did not initially have a track team. The principal at St. Mary's High School in Waltham, Massachusetts, however, had once been a successful track coach and finally decided St. Mary's should get up to speed. "The team he had coached before had gone to the Penn Relays and won the High School Mile Relay title there," recalls Larry, who joined the new St. Mary's team. "He said, 'I want you to see what it's like at the top, and the first race I'm going to take you to if you can average a certain time is the Penn Relays.' It turned out to be the first race I ever ran and it really opened my eyes. From that experience I began to realize the magnitude of the sport and just how good the other runners were. It really inspired me to focus and train harder when I saw how fast those teams were."

With a new focus and work ethic, Larry lowered his mile time to 4:28, good enough to be offered a track scholarship to Boston College. "It showed me that I had ability if I worked hard," he says. In college, Larry benefitted from racing against the top teams in the east and from the friendly competition among his teammates. By his senior year, a personal best time of

4:07 for the mile earned him the anchor position on the Boston College Distance Medley Relay team, which would compete at the Penn Relays. "In my senior year the big deal to me was still the Penn Relays," he recalls. That's where track was in those days. And as it is today, the premier race for a team to win was the Distance Medley Relay. It was the epitome of a race to be in, and the most exciting thing to try to win."

The Boston College team, made up of three New England kids and one from New Jersey, arrived at the University of Pennsylvania's Franklin Field clearly not one of the favorites. "We didn't know what we could do," says Larry. "We were up against teams we had never beaten, so there was no discussion on our part coming into the race that we could win it. The Distance Medley teams were always loaded with the best guys on each team. Fordham had already won the 4 x 1 mile relay at the meet; Georgetown and local favorite Villanova were also there. Pat Traynor, a local boy from Philadelphia, was running the anchor leg for Villanova. He would eventually make the Olympic team in the steeplechase and run under four minutes for the mile; he was one of their big stars.

"Jim Owens led off the first leg for us (880 yards or a half mile) and came home with the lead pack," says Larry. "Then we had a kid named Bob Giovey who held his own in the 440 (quarter mile) and brought the baton in even with everybody else, including Villanova and Georgetown. He handed off to Phil Jutras for the 1320 (three-quarters of a mile) who ran a terrific leg. Phil beat Villanova and every other team to give me a five- to ten-yard lead.

"So I get the baton for the anchor leg (one mile) and I knew it was all on my shoulders. I had faced these guys before and I knew I had to be unrelenting in my pace. In addition to Traynor for Villanova, Fordham's anchor was a 1:47 half miler, so I had to worry about his speed. When you're up against a 1:47 guy and your best time in the half-mile is 1:52, you don't want him near you. I felt that if I let them catch up and take the lead, they would rely on their speed and outkick me and everybody else. So I vowed that I was just going to go hard from the gun and if I died, I died. I was going to try to open up enough of a gap to try and break their will. Then they would figure they weren't going to get me and just battle it out for second place."

Franklin Field's track, like most tracks in those days, was composed of speed-killing, hard-packed cinder granules. It would be many years before the speedier, hard rubber surfaces would be commonplace on college tracks. As Larry remembers, "It was a slow, chewed-up cinder track. It was lumpy and soft, and you could feel it. I got the baton and I thought, 'Wow, this is so slow.' Imagine all the spikes that had been through that with race after race."

But though the cinder track may have been a hindrance, Larry discovered an element of that race that worked in his favor. "I went out in the first lap in 57.8. When I got to the backstretch on that lap, I noticed it was a Villanova crowd that day in the stands; there wasn't anyone cheering for Boston College or any of the other teams. As I passed groups of Villanova fans, it would be maybe five or six steps later that I would hear them cheer: 'C'mon, Pat. C'mon, Traynor.' So I knew exactly where he was in the race. That was the key thing. I can't overemphasize how helpful that was. I could listen to the crowd reaction and measure how many steps I was past them before they started yelling for Traynor. I never thought of that as being something that would be helpful but as I was running the race it was a huge revelation; I could tell right where everybody was.

"I tried to keep the pace high, but obviously I couldn't keep up 57.8. I went by the half mile in two minutes flat. By the time I came around on the second lap at the 660-yard mark there were definitely fewer fans yelling for Pat; by then it wasn't until I was eight or nine steps beyond them that I heard cheering for him. And I didn't hear anybody yell for any runners from the other teams. I went by three quarters in 3:04 and change and realized I had never gone out that fast in my life. I had no idea what was going to happen that last lap. I was just hoping I could hold it together reasonably well. My best time trial at three quarters of a mile was three minutes flat, so there I was within four seconds of that and trying to hold on. I kept pushing and I didn't save anything at that point. When I got to the backstretch on the final lap I heard no cheering for anybody behind me, but I knew the last 200 yards was going to be ugly.

"So I was doing my best to keep my form, thinking about anything inspirational that would help me hold it together, and praying that I could get to the finish line for Boston College and get my Penn Relays watch (the traditional prize given to the winner). With a hundred yards to go I didn't hear the crowd roar for anyone else, and nobody was gaining on me. I remember I hit the finish line with a big smile on my face and that photo showed up on the front page of the sports section in my local paper, *The Boston Globe*, the next day. Boston College had not won a Penn Relays title at any distance in thirty years, and we did it with three New Englanders and one kid from New Jersey taking on the great Distance Medley Relay teams. I was really proud of our team, and I was thrilled to survive that last lap and beat those guys because they were all talented anchors. I took a chance. I was pleased to be willing to lay it all on the line to run the race I had to run."

Larry didn't know it at the time, but that race was just one of several events that would happily connect him with the Penn Relays for more than five decades. For while his collegiate running career was coming to a close, his future in broadcasting was not too far off in the distance. Reflecting on the significance of that event in his life, Larry says, "Not only did I run my first race there, but four years later we won the Distance Medley Relay title, and after many years of announcing the meet I hosted the 100th anniversary of the Penn Relays for ESPN." The anniversary weekend was topped off by Larry being presented the Lifetime Achievement Award as a Penn Relays commentator, the first time the annual award was ever given to a broadcaster.

But the Penn Relays was not finished with Larry Rawson just yet. Recently he was invited back to present the prized watches to the winning Distance Medley Relay team (Penn State) to commemorate fifty years since his Boston College team won their title. "If I ever decide to be cremated I'd like to have some of my ashes spread at the Penn Relays at Franklin Field," he jokingly says. "This event has played a huge role in my life. It has all these little bits that have become touchstones in my career. It's just amazing how all these pieces became significant."

Running Tip: "Particularly in the second half of a race, think of someone who inspired you in your life. I would typically bring to mind one great coach I had for awhile or my family. They usually inspired me to the best heights I could achieve on the track."

Kenley Ferrara Potts

"My best race was actually my worst race. I did everything wrong." Surprisingly, Kenley Ferrara Potts was not a new runner but a running coach and pacer who had helped countless runners achieve their running goals. When she finally took a break from pacing duties to run a race by herself, she failed to take her training or the race seriously, and suffered the consequences. The silver lining from her embarrassing performance was being able to use what she learned to teach future runners what *not* to do in a race.

As a cross-country runner in high school, Kenley disliked the pressure of competition. "I just wanted to do my own thing and run at my own pace," she says. "In college I just did fun runs." When she moved to New York City she fell in love with running in Central Park and started working for Nike in their marketing department for all running-related events. "When Nike implemented their first New York City Half Marathon in 2006, they needed pacers as part of the Nike Pacer's Program, and they asked me. Something just clicked," she recalls. "I loved it and I loved the runners. It was really cool to cross the finish line with people who had never run that distance before.

"The New York Marathon was the first big race I ever decided to run on my own instead of as a pacer," she says. It was also the first time she would ever attempt the 26.2-mile distance. But Kenley's coaching responsibilities came first. While taking her sixty Nike runners through a daily training regimen geared toward completing their first marathon in four hours and thirty minutes, Kenley had set her sights on finishing that same race fifty minutes faster to qualify for the Boston Marathon. "That was my biggest mistake," she recalls. "The whole summer I was doing training runs with them at their pace, but planning to run the upcoming New York City Marathon on my own and qualify for Boston. I don't know what I was thinking. Even though I put in the mileage I needed, it was never at the right pace. You can't train at a 4:30 pace and think you're going to run a 3:40 marathon; that's one of the biggest marathon training rules I broke."

Kenley also admits she didn't practice what she preached when it came to strength training and injury prevention exercises. "I'm really into pre-hab instead of re-hab and I was making my runners do stretches and everything else they were supposed to do, but wasn't doing it myself. I had become used to the half-marathon distance and I thought the marathon was going to be just more of the same, so I didn't need to do anything special. So, I wasn't doing warm-ups, I wasn't jogging before the start, and I wasn't doing dynamic stretching or any strengthening exercises. I was saying, 'Do this, do this,' and my runners were all listening. But they were first-time runners and I had been a runner for so long so I didn't think I had to do it. I ended up with an awful hip flexor that stayed with me all through training and all through marathon day, and it led to issues with my hamstring and my knee."

Besides dismissing the recommended "pre-hab" routines, Kenley ignored the workouts that would prepare her body to run at her desired Boston Marathon-qualifying pace. "I was doing beginning marathon training with my Nike runners, and I really should have been doing speed workouts, hill workouts, and tempo runs," she says. "I should have been running 20- to 22-mile long runs but I wasn't. We never ran more than eighteen miles at a slow pace, and that's really what got me. To jump up to a faster 3:40 marathon pace on race day was very difficult to maintain."

Race day arrived and Kenley had met with her Nike runners at the start before setting off on her own. "In the beginning everything was exciting because I was with all the runners and we were talking and eating and we had been out the night before to celebrate. I wanted to go with a pace group because I know it really helps all of my runners, so I started out with the 3:40 pace group (pace groups are led by an experienced runner who is responsible for running the race at a predetermined pace for the group to follow.) At first I was totally fine. I felt my hip flexor the whole time but I made it to mile thirteen on pace. But once I hit mile thirteen, I bonked. Suddenly I wasn't feeling that great and my stomach wasn't feeling that great. Usually I'm really talkative but I wasn't talking to anyone in my pace group and I slowly started to fall behind."

From there things went from bad to worse for Kenley, both physically and mentally. "I ended up walking for a really long time," she recalls. "One of my close friends who is also a Nike pacer was supposed to meet me at mile fourteen, and I was dressed completely in yellow so she could find me. Not only was I feeling terrible but I stood out like a sore thumb. I got sick to my stomach many times because I was putting in so much that my body was not used to and that I had not practiced taking during training. I was overdrinking Gatorade and I was taking anything I could, anything anybody was handing me. I was so upset and overwhelmed because things were going so badly that I ate a bagel, a banana, and salt tablets, none of which I was used to eating on the run. I had blisters and chafing too. I knew about an anti-chafe balm but hadn't bothered to use it.

"Everything we ever learned about mental toughness my friend was trying on me, and nothing was working. We were just walking and jogging and walking. All I wanted to do was quit and every subway station I saw I wanted to enter. If I didn't have her I don't know what I would have done." Then came perhaps the most discouraging point in the race, when the slower Nike pace groups caught up with her. "One by one every pace group passed me and I thought how embarrassing that was because I'm supposed to be the coach, and I can't even do what I've been telling everyone else to do. I thought after that I had no business working for Nike. I wouldn't be able to show my face at the next meeting. It was all my own doing. I never respected the distance and that is what I deserved."

When Kenley finally arrived in Manhattan her family was

somewhere on the sidelines waiting to cheer her on. "I passed my family and they saw me walking, and it was just awful. I finally came to mile twenty-five and wanted to finish running, and then afterwards when I caught up with my family I was in such pain. Usually after every race there's a big party and all the runners and family members get together, but I just went home and went to sleep."

Kenley commiserated with some of the other Nike pacers who related similar experiences. "We're supposed to know what we're doing and we didn't do it," she says. "Their advice? Train our runners but also train for yourself and it will be okay. They were very supportive. Having close friends to get me out of my funk was a turning point for me. After that I used as many sources as possible to learn the right way to train for a marathon."

Eventually Kenley took on a more formal coaching role at Nike, and when training began for the spring marathons she was able to pass on to her students what she had learned from her marathon. "Before, I wasn't doing any of the pre-hab things so I ended up having to re-hab. I didn't want my runners to have to do that because injuries can be prevented. Before each training run I took everyone through a fifteen-minute regimen of warm-up, stretching, core training, and strides, making sure they exercised specific parts of the body. It was more than we had ever done before, and the positive feedback from runners was overwhelming. It was amazing to see three hundred runners standing in Central Park all doing the same thing."

In addition, Kenley would reinforce the importance of training at the correct pace, sticking to a schedule, pre- and in-race fueling with familiar foods and beverages, and respecting that 26.2-mile distance. Perhaps the most important lesson she tries to instill in her first-time marathoners is that "it's all about crossing the finish line and wanting to run a second one. It's not necessarily about hitting a goal time or running your fastest race ever. I really think that when you cross the finish line it changes your life completely."

Looking back on her first marathon performance, Kenley suggests that everyone needs to be humbled. "The marathon is not just a fun run, it's very serious. I'm glad it happened early in my coaching career because I wouldn't be the way I am today without it; it made me a better coach. The 2007 New York City Marathon was my best race because I took everything that I did incorrectly before and during the race and used it to help my Nike runners and private clients to successfully race hundreds of marathons. My runners truly benefitted, and their successes have always felt like my successes too."

Running Tip: "Constantly stay positive. As soon as a negative thought comes into your mind during a race, punch it out and substitute it with something positive from a previous run. When it comes down to it, your legs can do it. It's your mind that can't, so you have to keep on top of your mind at all times."

Hyleas Fountain

To an aspiring Olympian, finishing fourth at the Olympic Trials is what nightmares are made of. Because only the top three in an event make the US Olympic team, those who finish fourth are *this close* to achieving their dream, then left on the outside looking in. More than any others in the competition, they will spend the next four years asking themselves, "What if?" No one knows that feeling better than heptathlete Hyleas Fountain, who waited four long years for another crack at making the podium.

The heptathlon is a two-day, seven-event competition in which women earn points based on how well they run, jump, and throw. During the event's first day, athletes compete in the 100-meter hurdles, high jump, shot put and 200-meter run, in that order. The second day consists of the long jump, javelin throw, and 800-meter run. The heptathlon (formed by the Greek words for "seven" and "contest") made its Olympic debut in 1984.

"I didn't actually get interested in the heptathlon until 1996 when I first saw Jackie Joyner-Kersee on TV," says Hyleas. "I really looked up to Wilma Rudolf during my elementary and middle school years, and then I found out about the heptathlon and how Jackie Joyner-Kersee was doing such amazing things. I was already doing a bunch of events in school in my hometown of Harrisburg, Pennsylvania, like the softball throw, standing long jump, 440-yard run, and all the relays, so already I was getting well-rounded." Once Hyleas entered high school she excelled in other sports as well, including field hockey, basketball, and cross-country, but what she really wanted to do was the heptathlon. Unfortunately, the event was not offered to high school students in the state. "In my senior year I was talking about doing the heptathlon when I went to college, but everyone thought I was crazy," says Hyleas. "They said, 'Nobody ever wants to do that!' When I got to college I did my first heptathlon and I've loved it ever since, and everybody *still* thinks I'm crazy."

Hyleas was a two-time junior college champion in the heptathlon, and later the NCAA heptathlon and long jump champion while attending the University of Georgia. But when she competed at the 2004 Olympic Trials just after graduation, she missed out on making the Olympic Heptathlon team by one place. The dream she had since the age of seven of representing the United States in the Olympics had to be put on hold for another four years. "I believe God does everything for a reason. In 2004 God put me close to it to let me know I had to work a little bit harder, and that there were still some things I needed to learn. I learned a lot in four years."

Through the rigors of training and competing at the highest level in her sport, Hyleas learned that one has to first pay her dues. "The main thing I tell younger competitors now is that you have to be patient," says Hyleas. "Success is not something that is going to come overnight. It's just something you have to be willing to be around a long time in order to medal. In the history of the event, there are only two from the US who have medaled, so that just shows how hard it is. Experience means everything. If you're just starting out you don't know how to mentally get through each event, and the first event (the 100-meter hurdles) can sometimes make or break you. I've seen girls have a bad hurdle race and let it carry out through the rest of the competition. You have to have your moment of either sadness or joy and then move on to the next event. There are seven events and seven different times you can be taken down, but you can always make up points in other events."

Hyleas also became serious about nutrition and how it can affect her body and her performance. "I could get away with not eating right in college," she recalls. Only much later did she begin to understand the importance of how to fuel and refuel correctly. "Once I got together with a dietary nutritionist, I understood what foods work best for energy and what's going to work best when I'm competing, what's going to make me feel like crap and what's going to make me feel great. I just made it a way of life."

Her way of life in terms of training was modeled on balance in order not to focus too much on any one event. "I like to work on a very structured schedule. I know Mondays I'm going to have a sprint hurdle workout. Tuesdays it's going to be some type of shot put and interval workout. The workouts are not always the same, but I know what days I'm throwing and what days I'm jumping." Above all, Hyleas had to believe that those prescribed workouts would enable her to make a serious challenge for one of the top three spots on the Olympic team; that was her outlook going into to the 2008 trials in Eugene, Oregon. "I just had to let everything go and trust in my coach and trust in my training, and know that I've done everything I could to make the team," she says. "Going to Eugene I had lots of nerves. It was my second Olympic Trials and I didn't want a recap of what happened in 2004. I didn't want to finish in fourth place. My goal was to go in very confident. I told myself that there will not be any doubt in anyone's mind that I made the team."

If ever there was a confidence builder, it was Hyleas' performance in the first event on the first day of the heptathlon. "I started off the competition by breaking the American record in the 110 hurdles!" Her effort in the next event, however, was not nearly as impressive. "In the high jump I couldn't clear six feet but jumped 5'11". It was mediocre but it was okay. I didn't want that little thing to tear me up." Her next event, the shot put, was never one of her best. "I struggle mentally with the shot put, and my coach just told me to relax. He said I have a full minute to throw and that I didn't need to rush it. When you're in the shot put ring, one minute is actually a long time. So I got in there and relaxed and my very first throw was a personal best." A perfect end to her first day was her clocking another personal best in the 200, no doubt aided by her visualization techniques to relax and get in rhythm. "As an athlete I keep replaying and visualizing what I'm going to do," she says. A lot of my visualization is about the rhythm I need to be on. You might see some film of me with my eyes closed and I'm moving my hands in a running motion trying to catch my rhythm before a race. I was so relaxed and I was having so much fun. I had three out of four personal bests and after day one I was in first place. I was really excited but I wanted to keep calm and get back to the hotel. You really have to stay focused and understand you have another day to go."

Hyleas also had to get enough sleep, something she lacked in previous competitions. "In such situations I don't sleep very well and I really believe in acupuncture. I get it within hours before going to sleep because it puts me in such a relaxed state and helps with my recovery. I wasn't even sore the next day even though I exerted myself to three personal bests." The next day's first event, the long jump, is also her best. "It's something I can do very fluidly and not have to think about or be nervous about." The former NCAA champion in that event promptly jumped farther than she had ever jumped before, and followed that up by throwing the javelin farther than she had ever thrown before. "I kept my composure and my form was perfect and everything just fell in place. I only needed to take one throw.

"I work myself up so bad for the 800," she says, referring to the final event of the competition. "I was always a mental case when it came to that. I'm perfectly fine in training, but sometimes I would get so emotional about it to the point of tears. There are two laps and they are going to hurt. I always think to myself that whether I run it fast or slow I'm still going to hurt, so I would rather run it fast." Hyleas did not run a personal best in that race, but she didn't have to. By then she had secured a spot on the Olympic team. "In the heptathlon you aim to finish in the top five in each event," she says. "Going in I wanted to win every event, and I won five out of the seven. But you have to keep your composure the whole way through. You can be excited inside, but you can't let it show until you cross that finish line in the 800.

"I made my dream come true. I finally did what I had been

dreaming about since I was seven years old. Everything I had been through those last four years had been worth it. Going to the Olympics was awesome, but my best race was at those Olympic Trials. I had so many personal bests and broke the American record in the hurdles, and after that I had the chance to meet Jackie Joyner-Kersee. We talked like we had known each other forever, and it was just a very memorable moment for me. Also, my mom was there. She saw how heartbroken I was in 2004, and she was right there when I crossed the line in the 800 and she knew how much it meant to me. She was the one who got me started in track and took me to every track meet. Knowing I had my mom there, I really didn't need much else. 'You finally did it!' she said. I don't think I could have been more blessed."

In August of that year at the Beijing Olympics, Hyleas initially finished third to win the bronze medal. But later when the second-place finisher tested positive on her drug test, Hyleas was awarded the silver medal. She and Jackie Joyner-Kersee remain the only US women to have medaled in the heptathlon at the Olympic Games.

Running Tip: "Trust in your training. If you know you've done everything you were capable of doing and everything your coach told you, you should perform well."

Roger Robinson

Roger Robinson was a Masters World Champion who believed he still had one more good marathon in him at the age of forty-four. When the professor of English literature was given time off for Easter, it coincided with the Boston Marathon, a race he had never before entered. Roger knew he would need all the help he could get to make a run at the Master's record, so when he came to Heartbreak Hill, he enlisted the support of an Irish poet.

Roger grew up in England with the ambition of one day playing soccer for his country's national team. It soon became apparent that there were two impediments to that dream: "I wasn't big enough and I had no talent," he recalls. "I was one of the skinny geeks who couldn't do anything else but run, and started running cross-country at school when I was thirteen. I did pretty well but it took a good while. I had no immense talent and didn't win very much at school and university but just kept on working at it. I didn't make it to the international level until I was twenty-six." It would be another fourteen years, however, before Roger realized his full potential as an elite runner.

"Once I turned forty I was really running well and winning races as a Master," he says. "I won the World Masters 10K Championship and the World Masters Cross-Country Championship, but I didn't run a marathon until I was forty-one." By then Roger had moved to New Zealand for a university position. "Marathons weren't that important in those days; they weren't the be-all and end-all that they are now. If you met another runner you asked, 'What was your best placing in the National Cross-Country Championship?' That was how you identified each other either in England or New Zealand. You never bothered to say, 'What's your best marathon time?' But with the American running movement in the late 1970s and the rise of the New York City Marathon, that distance was becoming significant. I was in America in 1980 and ran the marathon and realized then that this was the most important thing at that point in terms of what really counted in running. It was where the competition was and how you could establish yourself."

In 1981 Roger ran a personal best marathon in Vancouver, but as the years passed he admits not being sure how much longer he could expect such stellar results. "At age forty-four I was beginning to slow a bit," he says. "My times in the 10K were beginning to drop. But I had a good New Zealand summer of training and had done quite a bit of speed work and got some miles logged. It just so happened that year that the Boston Marathon came at Easter, and I was able to get away from my duties at Victoria University for a week. I reckoned I had one more good marathon in me.

"In a race you need to strike the perfect balance between physical total effort and mental total control," says Roger, something one needs especially during the Boston Marathon's first mile, which is a barely perceptible downhill. "My race started somewhat dramatically. When we went through the first mile I thought I was running at 5:20 pace, which is what I wanted to do, but they called out 5:01. Then I realized the first mile is all slightly downhill and that's why people screw up in Boston—they go out too fast. There was quite a lot of downhill running early on so I shoved the brakes on and backed off and let people go by me and didn't worry. I just kind of switched off and decided I was going to run the race I wanted to run. I wanted to try to run a 2:20, which means I wasn't going to go any faster than seventy minutes at halfway. Going out too fast was the danger, so I tried to detach as much as possible in those early miles."

Another issue on his mind was the nasty weather the runners encountered and had to endure throughout the entire 26.2 miles. "It was a terrible day," he recalls. "Howling cold wind and rain and sleet, and we had a headwind for most of the way. People were putting oil on themselves and wearing all kinds of weather gear. One of the keys on that day was finding big healthy young men to run behind because of that strong headwind. I remember there was a line of three such runners wearing "Team Brooks" outfits, so I got in behind them and it was perfect. As I began to move up the field at about the ten-mile mark, I'd move from one to another and sit in behind them to block the wind. I got through the half in just under seventy minutes, so I got it right. That's what Boston is all about; you've got to control it. You've got to resist that temptation to go out too fast in the first thirteen miles."

Since he was at the halfway point in the race, Roger was about to learn about two other things that make the Boston Marathon unique: the exuberant cheering of the Wellesley College coeds, and the Newton hills. "From halfway on I was passing people because I had been running an even-paced race. And anyone running Boston for the first time has to remember the Wellesley women at that point in the race—it's an extraordinary experience. The noise they make, you can actually *feel* the sound! It's just amazing. That was a memorable moment. And then the hills start. Everyone talks about Heartbreak Hill but there are a lot of smaller hills, yet I passed people going up."

But it was coming *down* the hills that concerned Roger. "At that stage in my career my calf muscles were very suspect and they would often cramp and tie up and tear in races, so I had to be careful not to spring too high, especially when going hard downhill. So I was thinking of a line from a W.B. Yeats poem ("Long-Legged Fly") where he says to 'Practice a tinker shuffle, picked up on a street.' I was trying to shuffle and trying to control it so I didn't harm my calf muscles. So I was able to really go strong on the hills."

Once through the hills, Roger kept passing others, trying to stay protected from the headwinds while at the same time staying focused. "Always with the marathon it's being on that edge of being excited but not too excited," he says. "You have to find the right crest of complete focus and concentration. People asked me about the scenery at the Boston Marathon and I didn't have a clue. Mostly in a race like that, if you're going well, you're so focused. You're thinking about the next five strides, where you are on the road, how to get the best line, and where the finish is. It's commitment and intensity without getting overexcited and going too fast."

By then Roger estimated he was among the top two hundred runners. Where he was among his Masters competitors, however, was anyone's guess. "There were quite a lot of runners who had gone out fast and therefore were paying the price in those final five miles," he says. "If you can be coming through them competitively in the second half of the race it's a good feeling. But the problem with Masters running is that you never know where the others are. You don't know whether you've been beaten or not. You're just in the middle of the field and there's no special identification to indicate a Masters runner. Not until the award ceremony several hours later do you know for sure."

Roger's finishing time of 2:20:15 set the Master's record that stood for several years. When he crossed the finish line in thirty-first place overall, however, his thoughts were on the history of the race and of those who ran before him. "It was just that thought of Boston. There I was in one of the most historic cities in the new world, and that was arguably the most historic race in the world, and at that moment I was contributing to it and becoming a small part of it. I've always loved the history of running, and I was really conscious of running in the footsteps of Ron Hill and Bill Rodgers and my mate Dave McKenzie from New Zealand who had won the race in 1967. I had them very much in mind. The New York City Marathon has a different kind of magic but it isn't a historical one. Boston being that much older was something I really had an admiration for at that level."

Realizing the need to put on the brakes after a fast start, staying behind others to block the wind, making up time on the hills, and staying focused until the end, was the balancing of physical effort with mental control to which Roger aspired. "Those were all factors and nobody can do that all of the time, but on that particular day it went exactly right. In my career I was just on the edge of slowing down and that really was the last top-class race that I was able to run. I like to think I was one of the last nonprofessionals because after that the prize money came and people were running full-time. I was probably the last to hold that record coming off a genuine full-time job, so that gives me some pleasure."

It also gives Roger pleasure to visit Boston's Copley Square where a monument was erected for the race's centenary. On it rest the names of every winner in the race's history— including Masters winners—engraved in stone. "I take a look at it whenever I'm there just to make sure it really happened. It's the only way I know to get my name on a memorial without being dead." Few onlookers, with the exception of a professor of English literature from New Zealand, would recognize that the quote on the monument is from Tennyson's "Ulysses." It's a quote that seems even more pertinent for a Masters runner approaching the twilight of an elite career:

> *One equal temper of heroic hearts,*
> *Made weak by time and fate, but strong in will*
> *To strive, to seek, to find, and not to yield.*

Running Tip: "Be committed and get the best out of yourself as a runner that you can. Running adds such enrichment to your life and is so worthwhile. No one I ever met ever regretted being a runner."

Alexa Martin

Alexa leading the Dirty Girls Trail Runners

Alexa Martin coaches the Dirty Girls Trail Runners with some unconventional training methods and techniques. In a recent race where her students succeeded, she didn't fare as well, and had to use what she coached to get herself to the finish line. It was a tough ordeal, but at least she didn't feel the need to assign herself the dreaded "Essay Consequence."

In the fall of 2010, a series of attacks on women runners in her region in the state of Washington inspired Alexa and a few others to organize the Dirty Girls Trail Runners. "There were many women runners who wanted to run on the trails in the area, but there wasn't a way for them to do it safely," she says. So the Dirty Girls Trail Runners group was formed to provide an atmosphere of support, training, and safety in numbers. Alexa, a certified running coach, advocates trail running for the benefits it provides beyond the natural beauty. "Running on trails keeps the impact down on people's bodies, and being on the trails (rather than in public parks or on roads), helps runners avoid the self-consciousness that a lot of them have when first starting out. It makes them feel less competitive too. It's been a very successful thing with about fifty to sixty runners showing up every Friday morning."

In that group and among the other runners she coaches, Alexa sees students at all levels of ability, from those who want to train for a marathon or an ultra, to those who can barely jog a quarter mile. Alexa admits she once belonged to the latter group. "Running is not something that came naturally to me," she says. "When I started running I was an overweight asthmatic smoker. I trained on my own for about eighteen years but was constantly riding the injury roller coaster. I thought it was my body type or my mechanics or my asthma. Then I had a thyroid problem and suffered a neck injury from a climbing fall and missed six months of training. By then I was back to square one and barely walking again." Alexa was coached back to health by a friend who was an elite runner, and learned through that process that much of what she knew about running was wrong. "It wasn't my body type or my mechanics or my asthma," she says. "It was simply that I had no idea how to train properly. So basically for a whole year I ran without a watch, and when I felt like walking I walked. I no longer had a specific number in my head about pace either, and yet at the end of that year I was running faster than I had ever run before."

Unfortunately, the Sun Mountain 25K in Winthrop, Washington was to be one of her slower races. With a length of fifteen and a half miles, mostly above tree line, along with almost 2,000 feet of elevation gain, the race was not easy for any runner, much less one who had just recovered from a bout of anemia, like Alexa. "I had not been feeling great, but many of my students were doing it and I just wanted to be there."

Joining her at the start that day were ten of her women students and three men, known as the "Dirty Dudes." Most of the students running with Alexa that day were at her ability level, and she was able to stay with them for the first three miles. After that, she began having trouble. "One of the things that is tricky about coaching that I haven't been able to figure out yet is how to coach runners and also focus on my own training at the same time," she says. "It's a hard thing to be able to do. The last few months leading up to that race I had backed off on my training to focus on the coaching. At mile four I started to get that prickly, chilled feeling when I know it's not going well. Usually I get that feeling in the last several miles, but it's not a good sign to be experiencing it early in the race, so I decided to back off and let my runners go.

"I'm competitive with myself," she says, "but at times in the past I would measure my self-worth on how I measured up against someone else in terms of running performance, and that's something I completely coach against. I train my runners that we're all given different physiologies and it's about *your* point A to point B and not anyone else's. I tell them that it's the death of a runner to compare themselves to others because it's going to completely suck all the joy out of running. I don't even let my runners use the word 'slow' because to us 'slow' is a judging word. What we say is that someone is running a 'kind' pace rather than a slow pace, or a 'very kind' pace or even a 'compassionate' pace. And we don't talk about running a 'fast' pace, but a 'brisk' pace. There are a couple of other terms we use, like running an uncomfortably sustainable pace or a comfortably hard pace. I knew that for me in that race, an uncomfortably sustainable pace was not going to happen, and that I would be asking for serious trouble if I continued like that. So I needed to get to that point where it felt just comfortably hard."

The Dirty Girls Trial Runners are also taught "mindfulness" exercises, which not only involve encouraging themselves but talking to the ground below them. According to Alexa, "We tell ourselves that just because we're feeling uncomfortable doesn't mean something bad is going to happen; it's only temporary. And when things are tough, like when we train on hills, I have my students *thank* the hill because of what the hill workouts are doing for them. And when the going gets especially tough, I have them tell me something they are grateful for, like a teacher who inspired them.

"As my mental state started sinking in the race, I drew upon those principles. If you coach your students to do it, you have to do it yourself. I took stock of myself a couple of times. For example, was I giving up or was I doing the best I could given the circumstances? I assessed my breathing and decided I was definitely doing the best I could. There was an aid station at mile eight, and three of my runners were already there and looking strong. They used to be the ones who always ran their workouts too fast. It was a bittersweet thing to know that they had at one time been running at my level and I had coached them to be much stronger than me at that point."

Another technique Alexa uses is meant to reinforce a training principle with which a runner is struggling or is ignoring. It is a writing assignment called an essay consequence. "I assigned one of my runners an essay on the difference between healthy vs. unhealthy competition," she says. "He was comparing himself to other runners at the time. Another runner was given an essay consequence on the importance of rest and recovery when trying to rehab an injury—she wasn't listening to her body. That was something I was in tune with during that race; what was my body telling me? At that point it was telling me that my effort was the best I could do that day, and if I did a little bit more I would regret it.

"The toughest of the hills came at mile ten, and even the fastest runners sometimes have to walk it, which is what I had to do. I got up the hill and was pretty beat by the heat, and on the way downhill my mind was telling me that I didn't want to be there, that I felt awful, and that I couldn't finish. So I told myself I had to think of fifteen things I was grateful for. That's something meditation instructors teach—gratitude is a response to negative thinking. I drew upon that and it really helped. And I didn't have any push in my legs any more but I could still swing them. Instead of focusing on landing, pushing, then swinging my legs, I just focused on landing and swinging; that I could do."

Soon one of Alexa's other students passed her, but the way she responded said a lot about herself and about her pride in being a coach. "The old me would have been demoralized by that, but instead I was able to be happy that she was running a smart race. She had held back at the beginning and had not gone out too fast, and would then finish strong. She was doing everything I told her to do, so it was a war between pride in my students and my own self-pride, but in the end I was really happy for her. I stopped a few times and cooled off in a creek, which kept me from overheating, and I think that simple act was the right instinct. That and the other principles I learned helped make the race merely unpleasant for me instead of awful."

At the finish, all her students were lined up cheering for her, which helped get her across the finish line with a smile. "All of them were people I had introduced to running on trails, and now they love it and never want to run on the roads again. To see how far they had all come in the last year or two of their training made me feel really good. They learned the hard way about how to train the right way, and they are enjoying success beyond their wildest dreams. They had to quit comparing themselves to other runners, to focus on their own point A to their own point B, and they had learned to run slower in their training, which embodies one of the great paradoxes in training and running: that in order to get faster you first have to slow down. Every single one of them was eventually able to do that, and they have been able to run their best races ever because of it.

"It was definitely not a great race in terms of how I performed, but it was a great race for how my students performed. I felt like I was able to use a lot of things that I taught them to keep myself positive in spite of how I was feeling, and that was like a victory for me. At the same time it was very meaningful to me to have the runners I coached do exactly what I had taught them, giving them a great race experience."

Running Tip: "When you stop comparing yourself to other runners, that's when you truly improve. Run your own race."

Judi St. Hilaire

According to 1992 US Olympian Judi St. Hilaire, her best race was the Manchester Road Race in Manchester, Connecticut; she just doesn't know which year. And that's because each year was fun, each year was different, and each year was memorable, like the year she was passed near the finish by a girl wearing big ears and a tail. But the race was also special because it became a personal yardstick of sorts that chronicled Judi's life as a professional runner.

"It's a composite of different years," she says, "and it kind of followed the course of my career. I've probably run the race ten or thirteen times, from when I was a naïve road racer, to when I was better established, when I was sick, when I was an Olympian, when I was coming back from an injury, and finally as a Masters and post Masters runner." When Judi ran the race the field typically topped out at 8,000 runners. Now the organizers close registration at 15,000 entrants, quite a change from the twelve who completed the inaugural race in 1927.

Besides tracing the arc of her world-class career, the race is meaningful to Judi for other reasons, no matter the year. "The race has a lot of character," she says. "Its not five miles, it's 4.7! It's a loop that starts on the big square of a New England town, flat and fast along Main Street. Then you take a left and go up about a mile and a half of hills. The end of the hilly part is deceptive. You think you are at the top but you aren't because the course bends around the corner and there is always one more hill. I always liked to refresh my memory of where that hill is by driving the course the day before. Then, after you come flying down the other side you come around a bend and it's a long

223

straightaway to the finish, and the crowd is just incredible there. It's a tough finish even though it doesn't look like it because there's this little bump of a hill right near the end of the race."

The day the race is held every year also makes it unique, and the perfect way for professional runners like Judi to finish out the road racing season. "It is run on Thanksgiving, the time of year after everyone had done their serious racing," she says. "It's sort of like your last hurrah for the year before you take a break. I've run some gutsy races there and I've probably won the race four times and come in among the top three most of the time. And every year there was something different," she recalls. "One year we awoke to eight inches of snow, other years it's been raining, or bitter cold, or sixty degrees."

Even with being from out of state, Judi always seemed to feel at home at Manchester. "We really connected with the people there," she says. "You mingle with the locals the night before at a big spaghetti dinner. It is very relaxed and casual. The elite runners would sit at the head table and we would have to get up and talk. There would always be a lot of banter and teasing between us. It was nice to be able to joke with your competitors, but come race day it was very competitive. The organizers would usually bring in three to four really good women runners and maybe ten really good men. Some of the best races were the races where I got beat because it was honest, pure road racing. I think of a road race as gritty and dirty—no laps, no lap timers, the gun goes off and you just run. Over the years at Manchester there was this big Irish connection of runners, and even though I'm not Irish I felt like they adopted me. And the years when I was competitive, people on the course would know me and call out my name. It always felt like a hometown race for me."

Inevitably, all runners reach that point in their careers where they can no longer set personal bests nor sustain the torrid pace they once could. Perhaps the most difficult part is finally admitting it. "I remember one Manchester race I ran as a Masters runner," says Judi, "when I was reminiscing on what it felt like to be really fit and really fast, and then struggling with that emotionally when I was hitting that turning point. I realized even though my brain said I can still run that fast, I really couldn't, and I was trying to accept that. I probably ran a minute slower than I used to run. Having won it so many times and then going back as a Masters runner and just placing in the top ten was a totally different vantage point from which to see the race."

Judi saw the race from another vantage point years later when she returned, in her words, "as one of the joggers and sloggers. The last time I ran it I was not in very good shape, running at 6:20 per mile pace and having people in costumes pass me. That's what I mean as far as the race following my career. I ran it when I was no longer in shape and felt the tug-of-war that I should have been able to run faster but couldn't, and having some girl pass me with big ears and a tail on." Indeed, costumed runners are a normal feature of the race, as are bands that entertain the runners at various sites along the course, something Judi could finally appreciate. "When you're racing you can hear the music but you're not enjoying it," she says, "it's just something that's there in the background. But that last time I thought it was really cool, and I got into it and got into the crowds."

Still, it was an adjustment for Judi to be running with the crowd rather than leading it. "When I was competitive I was out in the front and there weren't that many people around me, but the last time I ran it there were just so many people. I've never really run in that environment before; it was a totally different experience. It was fun until the end when everyone was passing me; I wasn't used to that. It was painful, both emotionally and physically."

How difficult was it for the former world-class runner and Olympian to eventually leave the sport behind? "It's a process," says the fifty-three-year-old. "There were times I would struggle with it. It's more like an addiction. You're so used to doing it. When it's your career and it's in your blood and you're running twice a day and you have to wean yourself off of it, it's hard. But then the pace changes—you slow down. Then the distance gets less and less. There were times before when I had to reflect and ask, 'Why am I doing this?' But now I'm doing it for different reasons; I'm doing it to stay in shape. This year has been the turning point. Running used to be the first thing in my day I wanted to do and now it's not. Now I fit my running around all my other interests. I feel well-rounded now. And I'm in a good place with it and in a healthy place with it. It's a healthier attitude."

Happily, Judi can look back on her years competing in the Manchester Road Race as a reminder of all that was good in a career of running and racing at the highest level. "It's the one race that had a little bit of every race I've ever run, put all together in one package: the competition, the character of a New England road race, the mongrel distance, the people. I'm very fortunate to have that one race where I had so many different experiences."

Running Tip: "Racing can bring so many disappointments when you put so much preparation into it and don't get so much back in return. So I think it's important to keep a sense of humor and keep it light at times because you're going to have so many other opportunities to get the result you're looking for. I used to be really hard on myself, and sometimes you just have to let it roll and not take it so seriously; step back and appreciate running for what it's worth. When running becomes too serious you take all the fun out of it. When that would happen to me I would always think back to when I was a kid when running was playing and it was fun. I think you need to keep that playful element."

Bart Yasso

"I was limping pretty severely right from the beginning but was willing to go out and kill myself to get to that finish line, whatever it took. Even if I had to start crawling I was going to finish that race, and then I was going to walk away from competitive running." After a thirteen-year battle with Lyme Disease, Bart Yasso knew his running career was coming to an end. Some days the paralysis in his body was so bad that even walking was a chore. But he had waited thirty years to compete in what's known as the greatest foot race in the world and wasn't going to be denied. As it turned out, the man who has run more than a thousand races in his career saved his best race for last.

"Running probably saved my life," says Bart Yasso. "I was certainly going down the wrong path and not leading a good lifestyle, spending too much time with alcohol. At age twenty-two I needed some focus and running came along. I wanted to run just a mile or two to get in shape, and I enjoyed it so much I continued. After I did my first race I was hooked forever." Since that first race in the late 1970s, Bart has competed on all seven continents, run five Ironman Triathlons, won the Smoky Mountain Marathon, and twice cycled solo across the country. In 1987 he went to work for *Runner's World* magazine where he developed the *Runner's World* Race Sponsorship Program, an outreach program that helps sponsor running events. With the title of Chief Running Officer, Bart is a familiar face at races, seminars, and runner's expos around the country, coming in contact with elite runners on a regular basis. "I have the opportunity to meet the greatest runners on the planet, and the common thread among them has always been that the Comrades

Marathon is the greatest race in the world. I thought that would be the ultimate race for me."

Comrades is technically not a marathon but an ultra. With a length of about fifty-six miles it is more than twice the standard marathon distance. The race has been run since 1921 in the Republic of South Africa as a living memorial to the spirit of South African soldiers who fought in World War I. From thirty-four runners that first year, the field now has to be capped at 18,000, making it the largest ultra in the world. Year to year the course alternates its start-to-finish direction: the somewhat more challenging "up run" begins in the town of Durban and ends in Pietermaritzburg, while the following year will be a "down run," going the opposite way. If the hilly, 56-mile course does not seem challenging enough, runners have specified times in which to reach certain checkpoints, or be forced to abandon the race. Ultimately, any runner still on the course twelve hours after the start is not allowed to finish.

"It is the oldest and largest ultra in the world, and it's the greatest race in the world because of the spirit that's in the race," says Bart. "It's a race that changed the complexity of South Africa. I believe it pushed the needle on the abolishment of apartheid because black citizens were not allowed to run for many years. When black runners finally did participate, they flourished. They would be winning and placing in the top ten, and TV viewers would see white people coming off the sidewalk to give a black runner water or to encourage them to the finish line. At the time I first started reading about it I was just a marathoner. I didn't think about doing an ultra at that point, but eventually I did a couple of 50-milers." Bart's personal best at that distance is an amazing 6 hours and 11 minutes, a time that would place him among the elite finishers at the Comrades Marathon in a typical year. Two obstacles, however, stood in his path on the road to South Africa: one was political, the other physical.

"I had wanted to do Comrades for thirty years," he says, "but I didn't want to go to South Africa during the apartheid years, so I was never that serious about it. When I did get serious about it I got sick." Bart contracted Lyme Disease not once but twice. The second time was in 1997 when it entered his neurological system. "I got paralysis on the right side of my body and it beat me up pretty good. I was never the same after that." Years after apartheid was lifted in South Africa, Bart felt well enough to enter the race, but then a flare-up in the disease kept him home. "After that I just about gave up on entering and realized it would probably never happen. Then in 2009 I did a marathon just to see what it was like to run that distance with so little training. I was slow but I made it. So I thought it would be my last opportunity to run Comrades." Bart's application was eventually accepted for the 2010 race.

The race that year started in Pietermaritzburg for what would be a "down run," but according to Bart, that shouldn't imply it is an easy course. "There's so much uphill in the 'down' course you can't believe they call it that. They talk about Heartbreak Hill at Boston, but the hills at the Comrades Marathon make the Boston Marathon look like a joke." Bart learned about the spirit of the race from the very beginning. "The start of the race is very ceremonial," he says. "They play a famous South African freedom song (the "Shosholoza"), and when you hear that it's pretty powerful. Just think that no black citizens were allowed to run in the race until the late '70s, and then you look around and see that the race field is composed of 50-60% black South African runners. It's a lovely sight. To physically be a part of that, to witness that change, is very special. That's what I remember at the start, the sheer emotion."

Those powerful emotions remained with Bart throughout the race, but so did the pain. "From the start I was limping because my right leg was in a lot of pain," he recalls. "If I was a spectator watching, I would have said, 'Hey, buddy, what are you doing to yourself? This is crazy.'" Instead of criticism, however, he received encouragement. "I've never had such a connection to spectators like I did there. All along the road they cheer for you, and when you come to small towns the people actually sing to you as you run by. They pick up your name from your bib and attach your name to their song. It's a personal connection, and very moving. They're so happy you came to their country and happy that you're running their race and they want you to make it to that finish line. There's just something about this race that gets you." Encouragement also came from his fellow competitors. "You wear a bib number on your back that is color-coded with how many times you've done Comrades, and it includes your name and home country; runners in the race interact with you because of it. If someone came up to pass me, they knew my name was Bart, that I was from the US, and that it was my first Comrades Marathon. Then they would encourage me to make it to the finish."

While making it to the finish was indeed his goal, Bart was left to wonder what his strategy might have been had he competed at the peak of his running career. "If I would have run the Comrades Marathon back when I could run fast I would have been setting a goal to break the top 50 or top 100," he says. "But when I went over in 2010, I was pretty sick, so I couldn't think of anything except making it to the finish. It was going to be a chore to cover fifty-six miles at the pace I needed to make it in before they close the chutes down, but I knew mentally I could psych myself up somehow. All I wanted to do was cross that finish line. To get to the finish is what it's all about." Still, Bart had time to soak in the scenery, especially during the long stretches away from the cities and towns. "You're out in the country for quite a while," he recalls, "and I remember the scenery was amazing, just gorgeous. You get some great vistas from on top of the hills. I think the uphills actually worked to my advantage because I wasn't beating myself up as much, although they are pretty grueling hills."

All things considered, Bart's race seemed to be going as well as could be expected due to his conservative pace and the constant emotional support from fans and fellow runners. "So I thought I was running pretty well," he recalls, "but at the halfway point I got scared. I learned I was only twenty minutes ahead of the time limit. I had to start picking it up, but I also had to be myself and listen to my body and then parcel my energy out throughout the rest of the race. At the next few cutoffs I was doing pretty well in terms of time, but I never forgot that threatening feeling that I could be removed from the course." Nor could he forget the panic that came with 6.2 miles left in the race. "I did get freaked out again later on," he adds. "I got to the 10K-to-go mark and in my mind I thought it was ten *miles*. I looked at my watch and thought there's no way I can make it. I can't run ten miles as fast as I need to run before they close the course! But then I realized it was only 10K not ten miles, and at that point I knew I was going to make it within the time limit. Even if I never ran another step I was going to be happy crossing the finish line at Comrades and walking away from running.

"You finish inside a stadium, and it was packed with fans when I came in. It's just such a cool feeling, like they were honoring you for finishing. And it's like you always dreamed a finish should be. No one was trying to beat anyone; we were all trying to help each other out, supporting each other to get to the finish in time. It's not your typical, 'I'm going to outsprint you at the end' thing. People were just happy to be there, and happy to support each other." Those with aspirations to one day run the Comrades Marathon must realize how serious the time limits are enforced on the course and at the finish, in order to preserve the competitive spirit of the race. "They actually close the gates to the stadium at 11 hours and 59 minutes," says Bart, "and then they close the finish line right at the 12-hour mark. "It was heartbreaking to watch but that's kind of the allure of the race. When I crossed the line in 11 hours and 23 minutes, I wanted to watch people finish those last 27 minutes before they closed the course. I was barely able to stand at that point, but to be right at the finish watching all those people come in was so emotional. Until the closure it was really fun screaming at people to make sure they got in before 12 hours had elapsed. In the final 27 minutes before they closed the course, over 3,000 runners finished behind me."

The first ten finishers in the Comrades Marathon receive a gold finisher's medal. After that, the type of medal received depends on a runner's time. "I received a tiny copper medal, which I really liked," says Bart. "I don't have many finisher's medals these days because I like to take them to Africa and give them away as mementos. But my Comrades Marathon medal is something I will save for sure. In retrospect it was the ultimate challenge for me in running. I had to go deep into the well to get to that finish line. I've done a lot of racing, but with the condition I was in, that was as hard as it gets. But even though I didn't go that fast, it was a good feeling to walk away from the sport knowing that I didn't leave anything out there and that I was finally able to cross the finish line of the greatest foot race in the world."

Running Tip: "There are races that you should just enjoy. It's really about the experience. It is getting to that finish line and being happy you are part of the sport. It took me a while to learn that lesson. I was always trying to set goals and was trying too hard for so long until I figured out how to have more fun with the sport. I know some people that when they are not competitive any more they just walk away from the sport and never do it again. If I did that I would miss so much. Even though I slowed down tremendously, I've still got the experience of incredible races and meeting some incredible people."

Acknowledgments

I am grateful above all to the fifty runners who agreed to take part in this project. It was a privilege to get to know all of you through your unique stories, and to learn how and why one particular race became so meaningful for you. I know many will be inspired by the special memories you so graciously shared with me and the readers of this book.

A special thanks to the team at Diversion Books for the guidance they provided in getting this book published. To Mary Cummings for her initial interest in the project and her editorial direction; to Sarah Masterson Hally for her shepherding of the book through the production process; to Angela Craft for her enthusiasm in getting the word out; and to others behind the scenes for their valuable contributions.

It was a special pleasure and honor for me to take part in this year's Hope & Possibility Run in New York City, a race founded by Trisha Meili who is featured in this book. I encourage everyone to become involved in organizations such as Achilles International that can provide hope, encouragement, and a sense of community to runners of all abilities.

Finally, I am grateful to Stephany Evans of FinePrint Literary Management for her faith in me and her commitment to my work. I look forward to more runs with her in Central Park.

About the Author

Chris Cooper is the author of *Long May You Run: all. things. running.*, a collection of essays and observations to inspire, encourage, and challenge runners to maintain their passion for the sport as long as they live. He has been a runner for most of his life, with numerous road race victories and a sub-three-hour marathon among his achievements.

A graduate of Pennsylvania State University, he is host of the blog "Writing on the Run," and has worked in the fields of marketing and public opinion research for more than twenty-five years. Besides his interests in running and writing, Chris cultivates a passion for wine by working part-time at a local winery. He lives with his wife in West Chester, Pennsylvania.

CPSIA information can be obtained at www.ICGtesting.com
Printed in the USA
BVOW08s0616050215

386494BV00004B/4/P